BEST PUB WALKS in and around MANCHESTER

Lydia Speakman, Colin Speakman and Neil Coates

Copyright ©, Transport for Leisure Ltd

All **Rights Reserved.** No part of this publication may be reproduced, stored in a retrieval system, or transmitted in any form or by any means – electronic, mechanical, photocopying, recording, or otherwise – without prior written permission from the publisher.

Published by Sigma Leisure – an imprint of
Sigma Press, 1 South Oak Lane, Wilmslow, Cheshire SK9 6AR, England.

British Library Cataloguing in Publication Data
A CIP record for this book is available from the British Library.

ISBN: 1-85058-410-9

Typesetting and Design by: Sigma Press, Wilmslow, Cheshire.

Cover: Boarding a MetroLink tram at Heaton Park *(Chris Rushton)*

Printed by: Manchester Free Press

Contents

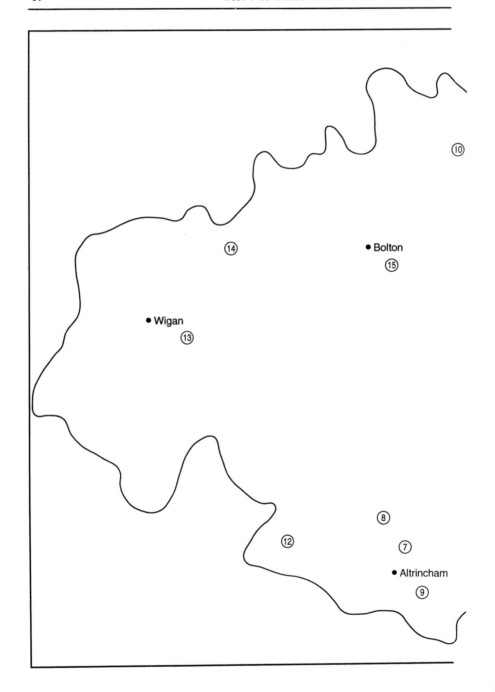

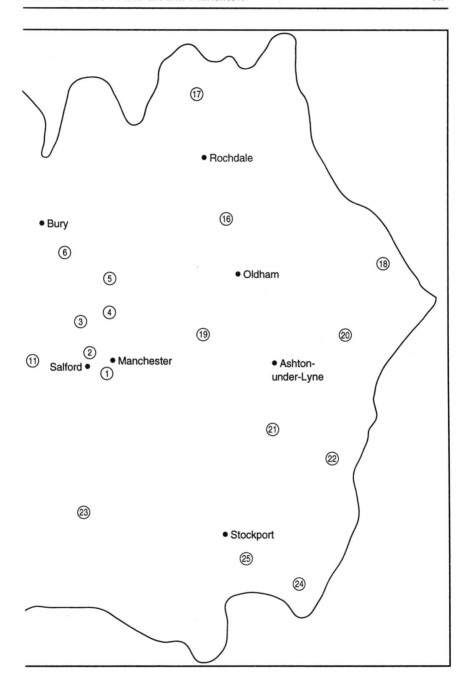

Manchester Cathedral: visited on Walk 1

INTRODUCTION

This book is about two things – it's about exploring the countryside, the paths and trails in and around one of Britain's greatest city regions, and it's also about enjoying a welcome pint of beer as a part of that walk.

It's not a good beer guide or even a good pub guide.

The 25 walks in the book have been selected for their quality and interest, and rambler-friendly pubs with decent beer selected wherever possible at the end or at least at a mid-point on the walk, if for no other reason than that it's nicer to enjoy a pint at the end of an afternoon rather than too early in the day.

Now what has really struck us while researching this book are two things.

First what we expected – the splendid heritage of pubs and excellent ale to be found in them throughout the towns and cities and even villages that form the Greater Manchester conurbation.

Secondly, a real discovery – the astonishingly rich heritage of countryside which is so accessible and yet still remarkably unknown even to people living in Greater Manchester within and around the edges of the towns and cities that make up the modern city-region. Some of this countryside is what one might describe as pre-industrial, little bits of rural Lancashire or Cheshire which have survived the massive spread of one of Britain's largest conurbations. Some of it might be described as post industrial, that is a landscape which only a generation ago was dominated by the mills, mines, engineering works, railways that served a great industrial and manufacturing nation.

For good and for ill, the world that produced that landscape has gone forever. The decline of manufacturing in England is reflected in landscape changes which are shaping the countryside of the twenty first century. Thanks to a combination of derelict land reclamation by local authorities, imaginative countryside management measures by both local authorities and organisations such as Groundwork Trusts, and the ability of nature to reclaim even the most desolate, ravaged landscape at remarkable speed, as willowherb, birch, sycamore and eventually oak and ash colonise waste heaps and riversides.

It's curious how our cars have at one and the same time allowed us to escape, at high speed, to ever wider horizons, and yet at the same time have resulted in us neglecting and even blighting the areas where we live and work. Why drive hundreds of miles every weekend to our overused National Parks, to and from the Lake District, the Peak District and Snowdonia, to walk on heavily eroded footpaths and queue at stiles, when so much splendid countryside and rich cultural heritage exists so close to home, often within a ten minute environmentally clean trip on a tram, bus or train?

This book is attempt to recify that situation – to discover that rich heritage of countryside which lies literally on the doorstep, and the equally fine heritage of friendly pubs and excellent, usually locally brewed ale which reflects the culture and communities of Manchester.

The Manchester Story

Manchester, that huge, sprawling conurbation lying across the western Pennine foothills, was built on the wealth of the cotton and engineering industries. It was the waters of the Mersey and its main tributary the Irwell, coming down from these same high Pennines, fed by many other tributaries such as the Tame, the Irk, the Medlock, the Croal, that provided the water to power the early mills. Rich exposures of coal provided the energy for the great steam powered mills and factories which still needed ample water for their processes. Pennine water also filled the pioneering canals which allowed coal and iron, those essential raw ingredients of the first phase of the industrialised world, to be carried cheaply and in bulk to fuel rapidly expanding industry.

But Manchester and her impressive ring of important sister towns – her twin city of Salford, and the boroughs of Bolton, Bury, Rochdale, Wigan, Oldham, Altrincham, Stockport, Tameside, Trafford – not only forms a city region which is still one of Europe's major industrial centres, but is also made up of towns and cities of fine Victorian public and commercial architecture, of densely packed terraced houses and huge post-war housing estates.

This is also a region which has always depended heavily on good communications – rivers, canals, railways, and roads, its townscape dominated by impressive 19th century railway viaducts and even more massive 20th century motorways. As a city region, Manchester reflects a dynamic culture – it is no coincidence that the city with the first public passenger railway was the first British city to reintroduce Metrolink – modern LRT or supertrams, and which has sought to relaunch itself on the world stage with an Olympic bid and an offer to host the Commonwealth Games.

Though hardly a city which conjures up images of quiet rural lanes, wooded river valleys or dramatic moorland scenery, such countryside can still be found. The region is also crossed by a quite amazing network of green arteries, many of them linked to the industrial and transport needs of the past – rivers, canals and old railways which go from the heart of the town and city centres into pockets of still surprisingly unspoiled hinterland. Many such routes and green ways between centres of population are explored in this book.

It's the landscape that provides the key to understanding the way Manchester grew and developed from a few scattered villages into a major conurbation.

Manchester was first settled by the Romans in 79 AD under the governorship of Caius Julius Agricola, who founded a simple early fort constructed of turf and timber. It was to become the base of a 500 strong garrison and an important crossroads and settlement as Mancunium, linked by excellent roads to the Roman settlements of Chester, York, Buxton and Ribchester. Today the foundations of one of the Roman forts can still be seen at Castlefields. After the Roman withdrawal, Manchester emerged as a small medieval town and trading centre (part of the Manor of Manchester), grouped around what is now the city's cathedral area.

During the sixteenth and seventeenth century, the textile industries became well established in South Lancashire and North Cheshire, producing wool and linen, and later cotton. Manchester became an important commercial centre, but also developed manufacturing and finishing industries. It was the eighteenth century that was to see the most dramatic changes in the town, and establish Manchester as Britain's first major industrial centre with the development of new methods of manufacture, the rapid expansion of the population from immigration and the development of new transport facilities which enabled the quick and cheap movement of raw materials and finished goods.

The pioneering Bridgewater Canal built by James Brindley in 1764 for the Duke of Bridgewater, to link his collieries at Worsley to the centre of Manchester, was not only a brilliant piece of engineering, but a major stimulus to trade. Its construction was swiftly followed by the development of a huge network of canals that was to link Manchester with the ports of Liverpool and Hull. Today, many of the canals remain as important wildlife habitats and walkways, making it easy to forget that the wharves and warehouses around Manchester were once bustling with activity and noise, as barges were loaded and unloaded. Canals remained the dominant form of transportation of goods until the 1850s, when the railways emerged as an effective competitor.

Manchester was also where the world's the first passenger railway station was built, with the opening of the Manchester-Liverpool Railway in 1830 and the city was to emerge – and remains – as the focal point as part of an immense railway network, linking Manchester to the rest of the region, the rest of England and now mainland Europe. The other major development to help put Manchester and its region on the map last century was the building of the Manchester Ship Canal in 1894 and its associated docks, establishing Manchester pre-eminence as a major port and trading centre in its own right.

By the end of the 19th century, Manchester was a proud wealthy city and borough, boasting a population of over half a million in 1901, compared to the 70,000 a century earlier. Such a dramatic increase both in population and size, could only have a major impact in the city and surrounding landscape and environment of the region. Large areas of cramped often poorly built housing appeared in once quiet villages on the edge of the town and along approach roads in long ribbon developments. Enormous cotton mills were built alongside once rural river valleys, employing huge armies of workers. Yet it was the period of immense civic pride manifested in the creation of public parks, grand squares and civic buildings and moorland reservoirs to supply water to the burgeoning towns. The nineteenth century was a time of new ideas;

for the wealthy manufacturing classes and new middle classes, the concept of free trade unrestricted by tariffs became a talisman to entrepreneurial spirit and wealth creation, personified in buildings such as the Royal Exchange and Manchester Free Trade Hall and in the wider commitment to civic pride represented by democratic local government.

For the labouring classes, Manchester became the heart of radical activity, both through the demand for greater democracy, by extending the right to vote and in demanding better working conditions. As the site of the Peterloo Massacre (1819) which saw the killing of campaigners at a rally fighting for an extension of the right to vote, Manchester was to become an important centre for Chartism, early trade unionism and later in the fight for votes for women.

Greater Manchester has remained a dominant economic force throughout much of the twentieth century. However, over the last quarter of this century, the region has witnessed a huge change in its economic fortunes, with the decline of many of its older heavy industries. This has had unforeseen economic and social consequences, with many people suffering unemployment but also huge areas of industrial heartland left derelict, with empty mill buildings, vacated workshops, crumbling factories and general degradation. But the region is fighting back.

In recent years Manchester has established itself once again as a major financial centre, specialising in the financial and services sector. Throughout the ten towns and cities of Greater Manchester, new uses have been found for older buildings as offices, apartments, restaurants and even museums. Computers now hum where steam engines once throbbed. New technologies have brought new hope. The environment, too, is being rapidly transformed. Canals have been drained and refurbished, and once derelict land has been reclaimed, spoil tips removed, trees planted and whole valleys renatured as country parks and areas of high quality countryside. This is a region which is using its resources and opportunities created by the past to shape a landscape and environment for tomorrow.

We hope this book might be a small contribution to that process.

Manchester's Beer, Brewers and Pubs

Writers on beer become remarkably excited when the words "beer" and "Manchester" occur together in print. Visions of (relatively) inexpensive pints of creamy-headed bitters and milds induce states of near-euphoria in even the most sober of commentators.

Often described as a Nirvana for Britain's lovers of beer, Manchester on the other hand has suffered more than most cities mid-to-late twentieth century from wholesale physical destruction and urban redevelopment, much of it as result of catering for insatiable demands of the private car for ever large wider and faster roads and more extensive car parking space. Together with the communities they served, several breweries, beers and pubs have long passed into history. Yet despite these losses, Manchester can still claim to be something of a real ale lover's utopia.

Several hundred different beers are available at any one time throughout the ten boroughs and cities which make up the geographical county of Greater Manchester, most of them in the increasing number of free houses, but a goodly number in the tied houses of several excellent local breweries.

The most widely known Manchester beer, thanks to a brilliant advertising campaign, is Boddingtons, the so-called "Cream of Manchester". Sadly, those with experienced palates report it isn't the beer it once was. It's not even brewed by Boddingtons any more, that company having sold the brewing function to Whitbread whilst retaining the bricks and mortar of the pubs, hotels and clubs. Whilst still brewed at Strangeways, you're now as likely to find a Boddingtons' handpump in pubs in Cardiff, Brighton or London as you are within sight of the brewery chimney – it's no longer a local beer and has lost some character in the process.

Another old stalwart among Manchester beers, Wilsons, is now brewed by Websters – in Yorkshire of all places – and is now all but phased out in favour of a blander alternative. Long gone, too, are other old favourites such as Chesters' Fighting Mild, Cornbrooks, Magees, Groves & Whitnall, Almonds and Oldham (still sold as such, but now brewed by Whitbread).

But what has been lost in terms of these national combines is more than made up for by the strong presence of local and regional breweries in the area. Easily the most celebrated is Joseph Holts' tiny brewery a mile or so from Manchester city centre. Until very recently only one of their pubs was outside Greater Manchester, and even now less than half a dozen of their hundred or so pubs are outside this boundary. Their reputation comes from the bitterness of the beers and the modest price, still well under £1 a pint in mid-1994.

No other brewery consistently matches this. The effect is to keep the opposition on their toes and prices more modest than in any other area of the country. Hydes (Moss Side), Lees (Middleton Junction) and Robinsons (Stockport) are Greater Manchester's other larger brewers, the pubs of each more or less clustering in their general area (i.e. Hydes in the south/south-west, Lees in the northeast, Robinsons in the south and Holts north-central and west), but all have outposts throughout the region. There are also a handful of brewery pubs with excellent reputations based close to central Manchester, including the Flea and Firkin (an old cinema on Oxford Road amidst the Metropolitan University) and the Kings Arms in Chorlton-on-Medlock. Also within the county is Oak Brewery, based in a part of the old Phoenix Brewery in Heywood closed many years ago by Bass, supplying a wide free trade in the area.

Of the big national breweries (Whitbread apart), Tetleys (Warrington) has probably the most outlets in the county, followed by Bass, Scottish and Newcastle and Greenall Whitley (whose beers are brewed by Walkers in Warrington). Particularly in the north of the county there are numerous Matthew Brown pubs, a trading arm of Scottish and Newcastle who took over this Blackburn-based company in the 1980s, thus also gaining the invaluable Theakston name and beers. Grand Metropolitan (Watneys) appear widely in the guise of Websters/Wilsons' pubs (although the number is decreasing steadily) and John Smith's houses.

Other well known names with a significant presence include Marstons (largely as a result of taking over small local breweries in the 1960s), Burtonwoods (based near Warrington, particularly strong in the west and northwest), Thwaites (Blackburn based, mostly in the Bolton-Rochdale areas), Banks's Wolverhampton and Dudley Brewery (largely via pub swaps and building new pubs) and Samuel Smiths (Tadcaster).

Part of the pleasure of consuming good local beer as well as the wide choice of real ales and beers (and from time to time porters) from throughout the British Isles lies in the immense variety of pubs in Greater Manchester. Whilst there's nothing to match the vast old "Gin Palaces" of Liverpool or Edinburgh, there's virtually every other kind of pub in Manchester here: from vast cinema/bank conversions to terrace house pubs, isolated country pubs at the end of rough tracks to ornate Victorian beerhouses, tile-fronted Edwardian edifices to time-warped back-street locals, medieval alehouses to quiet rural retreats. You'll find examples of just about all of these in the pubs described in this book.

Despite the blight of road schemes and redevelopment all over Greater Manchester, there are still a few areas where the bulldozers and the speculators haven't yet moved in, or where pubs haven't yet been transformed to themed leisure centres for yuppies, or upmarket credit-card restaurants where people in boots aren't welcomed. Central Manchester still has many excellent pubs. One area particularly worth visiting with or without a rucksack is Liverpool Road between Eccles and Patricroft in the city of Salford, virtually the last main arterial road in the county still largely unspoiled with a stunning number of excellent pubs; another is the Hillgate area of Stockport, a choice of lively pubs and Robinson's brewery tap en route. But of all the old Greater Manchester mill towns, Oldham is the one that has retained most of its characteristic back-street terraced pubs, particularly the area north and east of Mumps Railway Station.

An excellent guide to some of the most delightful pubs in the historic county of Lancashire, which includes most of present day Greater Manchester, is to be found in Peter Barnes' Traditional Pubs in Greater Manchester (a companion volume in the Sigma Leisure series), while the CAMRA Good Beer Guide remains the definitive guide to pubs with a real reputation among knowledgeable beer drinkers. Both have been invaluable to us in researching this guidebook, and wherever possible we've included CAMRA recommended pubs. On the other hand we've found some delightful, rambler-friendly pubs that aren't yet in the CAMRA guide which richly deserve inclusion. Enjoy them while you can!

Transport Matters

One advantage of writing this book is the ability to ensure that each and every walk in the book is easily and quickly accessible by public transport. There are two good reasons, even if you do have a car, for using the train, tram or bus:

First and foremost, alcohol and driving don't mix. The temptation to enjoy a beer – or two – during or at the end of a walk is perfectly understandable and what this book is all about. But if you then drive back through perhaps heavy traffic conditions, even if you are below the legal limit (3 units of alcohol), your efficiency is impaired – which could make all the difference in an emergency – and it isn't just you who is likely to be killed or injured. So why not, in a part of England which has excellent transport services, including the superb MetroLink supertram service, avoid the risk and leave the car in the garage? If you have no choice but to drive, then either stay on the waggon and leave others in your party to enjoy the beer, or keep strictly within limits.

Secondly, cars are now a major source of environmental pollution and congestion. Driving is stressfull. Again by using the train, tram or bus for all or part of your trip there's less pollution, less congestion and less damage to the environment – and to yourself.

Public transport is especially useful for point-to-point or linear walks, allowing a cross-country (or cross-town) walk without the need to return to the inevitable parked car. The nature of Greater Manchester's country-side with long green routes mitigates against circular walks. Point-to-point walks actually make more sense. Using the tram or train also reduces the risk of your car getting broken into in a remote place – car crime is now one of the fastest growing types of crime, with ramblers leaving their cars in remote places now a special target for criminals.

To make it especially easy, therefore, each of these walks has been planned with easy public transport use in mind. With rare exceptions, public transport was used in their research. Almost all the walks are based either on Metrolink, Manchester's superb new tramway system – so fast, frequent (even on Sundays), easy to use and inexpensive that a timetable isn't needed – or the Greater Manchester rail network from local rail stations where there are good local services. An off-peak Metrolink ticket is usually cheaper than parking in central areas, so use the tram to park and ride.

Remember too, that Metrolink also feeds into local rail services at Victoria, Piccadilly and G-Mex (Deansgate). However, some of these stations have only an hourly service at off-peak times (less frequently served stations have been avoided) so check times before you travel. Some local suburban lines don't have Sunday trains or a very infrequent service, but there are almost invariably plenty of buses along major roads to take you into and out of the city centre.

There are many bargain off-peak bus, tram and train fares, for travel within Greater Manchester, including Day Ranger Rail tickets covering the whole of the Greater Manchester Rail network and into neighbouring counties. For full information of such fare bargains and details of all bus and rail times ring Greater Manchester Passenger Transport Executive on 0161 228 7811 (0800-2000 daily); rail-only enquiries ring 0161 832 8353 while Metrolink enquiries are on 0161 205 2000. (Note that, from April 1995, all UK STD codes will begin with "01", so "061" will become "0161". However, BT are using the new and old STD codes immediately: you can use these new codes immediatel;y – you do not have to wait until 1995! *This book, therefore, contains the new STD codes.*

Summerseat, on the East Lancashire Railway: Greater Manchester's smallest station (Walk 7)

1. Manchester City Centre Amble

A walk around Manchester City Centre exploring some of the more interesting historic parts of the City including Castlefields, the Cathedral and China town

Distance: $3^1/_2$ miles (6km)

Map: Manchester A-Z Street Guide

Start and finish: Manchester Victoria Station (Metrolink).

The Pubs

Sinclair's Oyster Bar. Collectively known as The Shambles, the Old Wellington and Sinclair's Oyster Bar are two of the last timber-framed buildings to have survived from pre-industrial Manchester. The Old Wellington Inn was originally a shop and house. The building is thought to date back to 1328, though experts now suggest it is more likely to have been built in 1550. The house was once the home of the Byrom family. John Byrom, a poet and essayist 1692-1763, wrote the hymn 'Christians Awake' as a Christmas present for his daughter Dolly and also invented phonetic shorthand. Sinclair's, next door was already old when it opened in 1738 as Shaws Punch House. In the 19th century it became Sinclair's Oyster Bar and chop house.

In the 1970s, during an extensive period of redevelopment, The Shambles narrowly escaped demolition and was raised a few feet to be incorporated, rather incongruously, in the middle of a fairly hideous concrete shopping, car park and office complex. Restored and converted into a pub in 1981 with authentic-looking oak beams and antique fireplaces, Sinclair's keeps something of a Tudor atmosphere. Heretically in the heartland of historic Lancashire, its beer comes from Yorkshire – one of Britain's oldest independent Brewers, Sam Smith's of Tadcaster whose Old Brewery Bitter with its distinctive nutty flavour and stronger Museum Bitter is a favourite with many people. Open all day, food usually available.

One of only two surviving pubs on Liverpool Road, **The White Lion** has gained a new lease of life from the development of the complex of museums, canal-side walks and Roman heritage in this old markets area of Manchester. Nominally a Whitbread's House, its range of beers becomes ever more extensive, witness the burgeoning collection of pump clips. Much wall space is devoted to photographs, plans, map and artefacts relating to the Manchester Ship Canal, the centenary of which was celebrated in 1994; remaining areas are covered by fascinating collections of photographs mostly of old Manchester, paintings, and old lead and other seals and Guild Arms. Meals available most lunch times.

There are lots of other excellent city centre pubs on or close to this route to choose from – see Peter Barnes' *Traditional Pubs of Old Lancashire (Sigma Press).*

The G-Mex complex at Manchester's former Central Station

The Walk

Victoria Station was once the centre piece of the Lancashire and York-shire (L&Y) Railway and though its rail traffic is nowadays mainly confined to local commuter services (and a key Metrolink stop), the station's former glory is still reflected in its grand architecture, including the magnificent glass dome which crowns the station buffet, the gold mosaic lettering above the now redundant bookstall and a magnificent titled map showing the L&Y's long vanished and much lamented Railway Empire.

Walk out of Victoria Station and cross the road and turn left, and take the first right down Low Millgate and continue past the entrance to Chetham's Music School, one of the finest examples of a medieval manor house in Britain. Home of the De la Warre family, it was bought and endowed as a school and free public library in 1653 by Humphrey Chetham. In 1969 the School became the first National School for talented young musicians.

Continue along Lower Millgate past the plaque commemorating the founding of Manchester Grammar School to the main road. Straight ahead is the glass dome of the Corn Exchange. Cross the road and continue along Cathedral Street. On the left are a set of glass doors leading into the old Corn Exchange, now restored as a flea and bric-a-brac market selling a range of memorabilia and ethnic jewellery and clothing.

Continue along Cathedral Street and turn right into Cathedral yard and the main door into the Cathedral. The Cathedral dates primarily from the fifteenth century when it was founded as a collegiate church; it became a Cathedral in 1847 when the Diocese of Manchester was formed. There has, however, been a church on this site since 900 AD and a fragment of the Saxon church can be seen inside the Cathedral. The Cathedral was badly damaged by bombing in 1940, so none of the original stained glass windows remain; the 'Fire Window' commemorates the architect who restored the Cathedral. Look out for the finely carved misericord in the choir stalls showing medieval scenes and legends.

Retrace your steps and continue straight ahead to a main road. Cross the road with care and continue straight ahead along a pedestrian walkway to the right of an entrance to a car park. At the entrance to Marks and Spencer's turn left into Shambles Square and The Shambles – two pubs, The Old Wellington and Sinclair Inn, which stand like a small oasis in a modern concrete jungle.

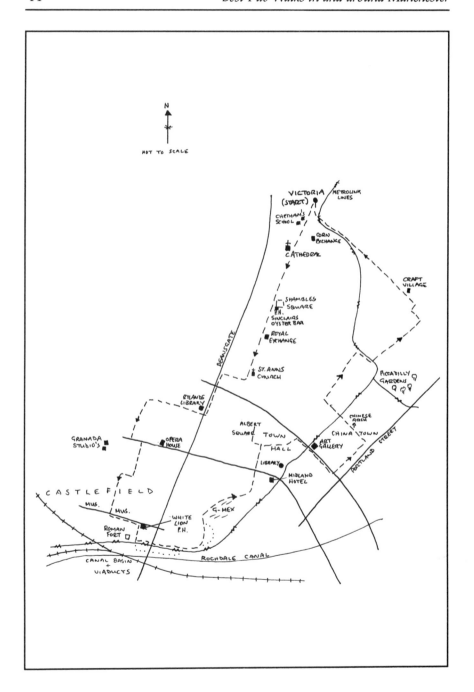

From The Shambles turn left through the pedestrian walkway and keep the same direction to cross St Mary's Gate towards St Ann's Square ahead. On the right is the restored Barton Arcade, a mini Crystal Palace built in 1871, housing a range of pleasant shops. A little further to the left is the Royal Exchange, once the home of Manchester's cotton exchange and centre of the city's commercial might. The Royal Exchange now houses its own theatre, an amazing structure of tubular metal cocooning a theatre in the round which sits strangely amongst its Victorian surroundings.

At the end of St Ann's Square is a statue to the Victorian Free Trader, Richard Cobden, and the Renaissance St Ann's church built in 1712 and designed in the style of Sir Christopher Wren which gives its name to the Square.

Walk round the right hand side of St Ann's Church and turn left down St Ann's Place through St Ann's Passage with its elaborate windows into King Street, renowned for its exclusive shops and summer buskers. Continue straight ahead down Boardman's Passage, looking up to admire the sculptured umbrellas overhead to shelter passers by from the rain. Turn right into Deansgate and then left.

Continue down Deansgate past the traffic lights to the pedestrian crossing opposite John Rylands Library. This fine Victorian Gothic building was built in 1890 by Enriqueta Rylands as a memorial to her husband John. The Library has one of the finest collections of early printed books and theological texts in the country including two Lutheran Bibles and several Caxtons. The Library was amalgamated with the University in 1973 and is now a research library open to the public.

Turn right down Spinningfield, past the offices of The Manchester Evening News and The Guardian. Continue down to a square and then turn left to walk past the Magistrates' Court to Quay Street. On the corner of Quay Street and Byrom Street is the County Court which was once the home of the political reformer Richard Cobden and later housed Owen's college, the forerunner of Manchester Victoria University.

Continue down Byrom Street passing St John's Street on the left, lined with fine Regency houses which is Manchester's equivalent to Harley Street, with each entrance covered in the brass plaques of doctors, surgeons and other medical practitioners. Turn right through an attractive park built on the site of St John's church and overlooked by Granada Studios. Go through the park and then turn left to the Manchester Museum of Science and Industry and the Aerospace Gallery. This is the site of the world's first passenger railway station, Liverpool Road on the Liverpool Manchester Railway opened in 1830. Inside numerous award winning exhibitions examine various aspects of Manchester's industrial past and future including a gallery on the city's sewage system through the ages, its engineering, railway, aerospace and computer industries. There's also a "hands on" science 'Xperiment' exhibition, popular with adults and children alike.

At the road junction, cross the road and turn left past the old Sunday school to the White Lion – another pub of note. Turn right down Coler Street to visit the Roman Fort. There was a Roman fort on this site from around 79 AD which was built by troops under the Roman general, Agricola. The first two forts were made of turf, but subsequent forts were built of timber. By the early third century a strong stone fort was built on the same site. Part of the northern gateway and part of the fort wall have been reconstructed to show visitors what they would have looked like. Recent excavations show that there was also a civilian settlement and traces of iron furnaces and of other industrial activity have also been found.

Just before the gateway, on the left, is a charming statue of a sheep and behind it a mural showing the history of the area from Roman times to the filming of Coronation Street.

Go through the gateway and then straight ahead under the four magnificent viaducts crowded above, the largest of which resting on iron pillars, was built in 1890, together with the Great Northern warehouse. Swing left to the old stone bridge towards Duke '92 (see walk 4) for a view of the Canal basin where the Bridgewater Canal and Rochdale Canal meet. Once an area of warehouses and bustling activity, the basin has been revitalised and cleared and is now the venue for a regular Canal barge festival and various other outdoor events.

Retrace your steps back under the viaducts, noting the wall showing archaeological layers of each of the Roman forts. Swing right towards the red iron staircase leading up to G-Mex. The less energetic can take the lift which stands alongside, but otherwise go up the staircase.

Walk past the Metro station and then head towards the back of G-Mex, now a major exhibition hall created out of the derelict Central Railway Station which was designed in a huge single span by Sir John Fowler in 1876. From here there are magnificent views of the city's skyline. On the left is the Great Northern Railway Company's warehouse and further on, the back of the Free Trade Hall, lined with white stone figures of famous singers and conductors, and home of the Hallé Orchestra.

At the front of G-Mex turn and go down Mount Street round the side of the huge Midland Hotel, cross St Peter's Street and continue around the back of the fine 1930s Central Library and into Albert Square, so called after the famous Memorial to Prince Albert which stands in front of the magnificent Manchester Town Hall.

Topped with a 280ft clock tower, the Town Hall dominates the city's skyline. It was designed by Alfred Waterhouse, and was opened in 1877, having taken nine years to complete. Inside, it is lavishly decorated with richly painted ceilings, fine sculpture and a wonderful set of twelve murals by the painter, Ford Madox Brown, depicting the city's history from the Roman fort at Mancenon to John Dalton collecting marsh grass – research which led him to develop atomic theory. There are regular tours around the Town Hall, contact the Tourist Information Centre for more details.

Retrace your steps and turn right down Lloyd Street into St Peter's Square. with its attractive gardens and statue to the Peterloo massacre. The Free Trade Hall is on the actual site of the massacre, where in 1819, 60,000 gathered to hear speeches for reform of Parliament by the radical orator, Hunt and Richard Cobden. However, the size of the crowd alarmed local magistrates who ordered the Manchester and Salford Yeomanry to disperse it. In the ensuing confusion which followed several people were killed or injured.

Walk straight ahead towards the City Gallery which has a fine collection of Pre-Raphaelite paintings as well as collections of early Flemish, Dutch, Italian and French works of art. Continue along Princess Street and then take the third left along Faulkner Street to walk under the magnificent 30 foot Imperial Arch and into the heart of China Town, an area of specialist Chinese supermarkets, restaurants and other businesses including a herbalist and acupuncture centre.

Turn left down Charlotte Street past the Portico library, founded in 1806 which specialises in 19th century books of literature and travel. Cross Mosley Street and walk down Spring Garden Street, through part of the City's financial sector, before turning right down Fountain Street past "The Shakespeare" pub with its fine Elizabethan carvings around its doorway, towards the Arndale Centre.

Turn right at Debenhams and then take the first right, Tib Street. Cross the main street and continue for a short while before turning left down Hilton Street and then first right down Oak Street to the Manchester Craft Centre built inside the old Smithfield and Fish Market. The Centre contains a number of Units selling a wide range of crafts from designer hats to jewellery and pottery.

Go down Copperas Street and then turn left, past the shell of a former fish market and then right down Thomas Street. Cross by the pedestrian crossing and follow a pavement alongside the Metrolink tram tracks down to Balloon Street. A plaque on the corner of Balloon Street and Corporation Street commemorates the site of the first manned balloon ascent in 1785 by James Sadler. Balloon Street leads directly back to Victoria Station.

2. Old Salford and The Castle Irwell Gorge

A walk from Castlefield through Salford's Crescent and Peel Park to explore beautiful green areas in the very heart of Salford.

Distance: 5¹/₂ miles (9km)

Maps: Landranger 109; Pathfinder 713, 724.

Start: G-Mex (Metrolink)

Finish: Heaton Park Station (Metrolink)

Access: Metrolink service to G-Mex. Car users should park near any Metrolink Station, transfer at Piccadilly Station to BR and return via Metrolink from Heaton Park Station.

The Pubs

The Crescent, on Salford's historic Crescent, is a slightly scruffy, unpretentious building but is one of Salford's most popular real ale pubs, specialising in a changing variety of excellent real ales, and noted for its food, popular with students. Not always open on Saturday lunchtimes.

The Royal Oak in Prestwich at the end of the walk is a pleasant, unpretentious pub, quiet and free of muzak, in traditional buildings which have been enlarged. It is situated on Whittaker Lane, an old lane in Prestwich which has kept something of its rural character on the edge of Heaton Park. Well kept Hydes' Bitter, Mild and Anvil Light on offer for tired ramblers – and all day opening, less then two minutes' walk from Heaton Park Metrolink Station.

The Walk

From G-Mex Station cross towards the G-Mex Exhibition Hall, but then bear sharp left following the metal signs on the wall to Castlefield along the walkway along the old railway bridge, past the car park to either the lift or metal steps down into Castlefields.

St Phillip's Church

Cross to the right hand side of the Roman Fort. keeping ahead down steps and past the little amphitheatre, past the Castlefield Hotel and onto Liverpool Road.

Continue to Water Street, crossing with care and turning right, before turning left at the next road junction, crossing over Princes Bridge. Cross the river and continue under the railway for the roundabout past Lloyd's steel stockyard, bearing right into East Ordsall Lane. Go under another railway bridge, but where the main road bends right, keep ahead along Stevenson Street, over a grassy bank by cycle way signs into George Street, heading for the elegant baroque tower of St Phillip's Church – a stately neo-classical building – on Chapel Street ahead. The large neo-Gothic church on the right is Salford Cathedral.

Turn left along Chapel Street, crossing Oldfield Road at the lights into The Crescent. The Crescent pub is 200 metres on the left; otherwise cross by the pedestrian lights at Oldfield road to the river side of the Crescent, and follow the river promenade road around to Salford University, noting the fine Regency Crescent of houses.

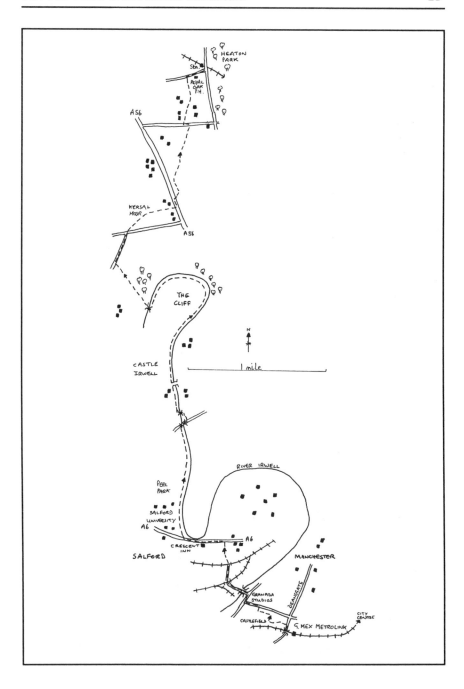

Just past the first block of the university is a red brick building, the former Salford Library – Britain's first free municipal library – now the Art Gallery and Lowry Centre – famous for its priceless collection of paintings by Salford artist L.S. Lowry, acquired when the Gallery was for many years a patron of the artist whose bleak vision of the industrial landscapes and communities of Salford in the inter-war years are an important social document as well as poetic and evocative works of art in their own right.

There is a signed path at the side of the first block down into Peel Park, named after Bury-born Sir Robert Peel, (1788-1850) Victorian Home Secretary, Prime Minister and founder of the modern Police Force.

Bear left at the first junction to join the main drive, keeping the same direction around the flower beds and along the avenue of ornamental lamp standards to the end of the park where a tall, stone pillar marks the height of the River Irwell in the Great Flood of 1866 – 8 feet 6 inches above its normal level; where the path ends, bear right towards the footbridge over the River Irwell. Do not cross this bridge, but keep to the same side of the river past the David Lewis Recreation Ground, following an avenue of trees and fence alongside the river upstream until you reach Frederick Road with its handsome bridge, emblazoned, in common with other Salford bridges, with the name of the Lord Mayor. To achieve immortality in Salford, you need to be Lord Mayor when a bridge is being opened.

Cross the bridge to the far side of the road to find a continuation of the path, signed Irwell Valley Way, along the far side, but the next footbridge across, again signed Irwell Way, takes you back to the west bank and a route past new housing (the former greyhound track) and a tall fence by the river to Cromwell Road by Cromwell Bridge.

Cross the road, but keeping to the same side of the river, make for the tall iron gates by high red brick walls here. These lead into the Castle Irwell Estate – again the Irwell Valley Way waymarks will reassure. The route follows a narrow, slightly overgrown tarmac track past new housing and into a great loop of land captured by the river which for many years was Castle Irwell, better known as Manchester Racecourse. Follow the river around into what is now a surprisingly lovely area of wooded riverside. Long views of the lower Irwell valley have a remarkable wooded appearance, the slender spire of St Paul's Church at Kersal making a striking landmark. The area on the wooded area on the far side of the river is The Cliff – see walk 3.

Where the track narrows and finally peters out, continue along the narrow path which follows the edge of the recreation land. Follow the line of riverside willows – Salford's name literally means the ford by the willows or sallows – as it curves around the headland, before eventually reaching a fine, single arched footbridge.

Cross the bridge, keeping the same direction to follow a narrow, tarmac track past blocks of flats. Where the track ends, past the entrance to The Cliff, follow the path which climbs steeply uphill over open land (fine views back into the Irwell Valley, and across to the tower blocks of both central Salford and Manchester), bearing left near the brow of the hill towards Oakland's Infant school at its crest. The path follows the fence around the outside of the school playground to join Oakland's Road.

Turn right in Oakland's Road, continuing to its junction with Moor Lane. Directly opposite is Kersal Moor, an area of sandy heathland, a delightful semi-wild open space rising above suburban Kersal. Cross to pick up a narrow, gravelly path which winds across the Moor, giving magnificent views in each direction, turning towards the Church of St Paul, now extremely close. The path goes over the brow of the hill and down steps to the right of the churchyard, soon entering a narrow way between the churchyard, Victorian houses and new factory unit, which shortly emerges into the busy traffic of Bury New Road by a garage at the edge of Prestwich.

Sadly, the last half mile of this walk is along tarmac, but at least it is mainly through quiet roads and leafy suburbs. Turn left along the busy shopping parade to the pedestrian crossing light opposite Kings Road. Cross into King's Road, but take the first road left, Rochester Avenue. This leads into Queen's Road. Keep ahead into Sedgeley Park Road, continuing for some 500 metres, passing the College on the right, to the busy Scholes Lane. Cross with care, turning left, but taking the first right past the letter box down the Ostrich Lane – named after the coat-of-arms of a local family. Follow Ostrich Lane for 250 metres to where it curves right past Bent Lane, taking the next, traffic calmed street on the left, Blackburn Street, before turning right into Whitaker Lane, soon passing St Hilda's Church on the right. The Royal Oak pub is on the right, near the end of the lane, and 100 metres beyond, at the junction with Bury Old Road is Heaton Park Metrolink Station.

3. Prestwich Forest and The Cliff

A walk with a few surprises – from suburban Prestwich down thickly wooded Prestwich Clough to the Irwell Valley and the recently established Prestwich Forest, taking in Agecoft and the riverside before exploring the mysterious Cliff and delightful Broughton Park.

Distance: 6 miles (8km)

Maps: Landranger 109; Pathfinder 713

Start: Prestwich (Metrolink)

Finish: Crumpsall (Metrolink)

Access: Metrolink – Bury Line. Motorists should park at any station and take the Bury line train.

The Pub

The Star (Robinson's) A pub in a quiet corner at the edge of The Cliff of almost rural character, early Victorian, white walled, with an outside ladies loo; family run, notable for excellent Robinson's Best Bitter and Mild, with Old Tom in the winter.

The Walk

The name 'Prestwich' comes from Anglo-Saxon meaning Priest's retreat, hardly the image of the present-day bustling North Manchester suburb which, though in the Borough of Bury, is very much part of the Manchester conurbation. Some older parts remain, as this walk shows.

Leave Prestwich Metrolink station by the steps and main entrance, turning left along the busy Rectory Lane as it winds past car park, shopping centre and school. Opposite the school playing field cross on to Greenhill, a short road with a wine shop in the corner, at the end of which a narrow entrance leads down steps to Bury New Road. Turn left to cross at the pedestrian lights, and continue left to Church Lane, following past the fine 18th century Church Inn, (John Smith's) but keep left at the church entrance to follow a narrow alleyway by the church-yard and overflow burial ground.

The Star Inn, The Cliff

Opposite the church tower, turn left down a narrow enclosed cobbled track which leads into Prestwich Clough. "Clough" is a typical Lancashire word for a narrow wooded valley. Follow the path as it curves right down steps to a footbridge – don't cross but keep directly ahead down the valley, following the stream through woods of mature oak, ash, chestnut and hawthorn. Keep ahead for just under a half mile to where the woods open out, but about 100 metres before a field gate ahead, look for a wooden gap stile left which leads to a narrow path winding through the woods. Follow it over a narrow stream, keeping the same direction with the four huge cooling towers of Agecroft Power Station ahead on a broader track which eventually joins a dirt track by a curious little brick tower ahead. Continue ahead through groves of willow trees, past narrow ponds. This area forms part of the new Prestwich Forest, a project linked to the Croal-Irwell partnership to regenerate and re-naturalise this section of the valley. A small area of informal parkland, Drinkwater Park, forms the southern end of the Forest, as the track emerges at a car park by Agecroft Bridge on the busy A6044.

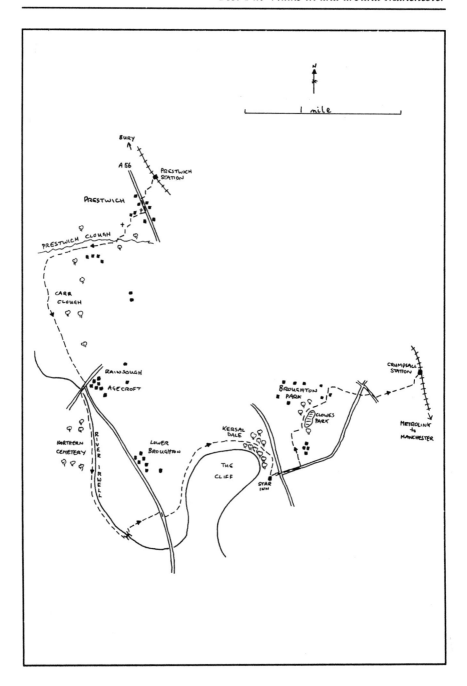

Turn right over Agecroft Bridge into Salford and cross the main road with care, to follow the path signed to The Cliff that follows the grassy bank between Agecroft Cemetery and the River Irwell, pleasant easy walking, past the cemetery and a chemical works to a small area of grassland and girder footbridge over the river. Follow the track between high fences between the playing fields as it turns left then right to Littleton Road, at a small parade of shops. Turn right, following the Irwell Way signs, for 100 metres to the pedestrian lights which lead into Northallerton Road, keeping left at the end along Rushley Road and to the concrete fence behind houses along the riverside. At the end, a gate leads to the riverside path and the footbridge used by Walk Two, but this time keep straight ahead along the riverside into The Cliff, keeping ahead past the riverside trees and across attractive open space.

The Cliff is a fascinating part of old Salford. Originally grand Victorian houses and their gardens covered the wooded slopes ahead. However, a series of landslides in the 1920s and 30s caused the houses to be abandoned and their ruins and their gardens have remained as a semi-wild area ever since.

Boardwalk through woods at The Cliff

A stile leads into the woods, with a board walk allowing the rambler to cross marshy ground dry shod. The path soon climbs uphill, past intriguing fragments of long vanished walled gardens, and mature trees, eventually bearing right to enter the truncated stub of Great Clowes Street where if you look carefully on the setts on the left as the narrow enclosed footpath emerges by surviving houses, you'll see tram tracks – long pre-dating Metrolink – vanishing into oblivion.

At the junction bear right along Lower Broughton Road where soon, past a couple of atmospheric Victorian villas and Hope Street, you'll find Back Hope Street on the left with, to the right, the delightful Star Inn. If the Star isn't open, then the Horseshoe directly opposite, also serving Robinson's Best Bitter, almost certainly will be. This is also an interesting pub in its own right, and has in recent years been in the CAMRA Guide.

To complete the walk, return to the Great Clowes Street junction, this time walking ahead along Cliff Crescent onto Bury New Road. Cross at the crossing into Northumberland Street, taking the second road on the left, Leigh Road, continuing through pleasant suburbs past its crossing of Broom Lane to Brantwood Road. Turn right here, but some 80 metres along Brantwood Road, two tall red brick posts topped by roundels mark the entrance to Broughton Park on the left.

Broughton Park is a jewel. A tiny public park, it is basically a lake fringed by trees with, as you look from the lake-side, the image of the tall Gothic spire of the United Reform Church mirrored in the water.

Broughton Park lies at the centre of Manchester's Jewish Community and you are likely to hear Yiddish or Hebrew being spoken as well as noting some distinctive head-wear among the families enjoying the little park and its wildlife.

Follow the lake around clockwise to the left, ignoring the next (main) entrance. Pass the playground, go over the bridge of the feeder stream, and turn left at the next junction, then left again in Water Park Road. Pass the sadly overgrown ruins of the United Reform Church on Hall Park Road to Upper Park Road. Right here to cross Leicester Road, keeping ahead to Cheetham Hill Road at the very top of Cheetham Hill Village. Cross at the pedestrian crossing and just to the right is Seymour Road.

Follow Seymour Road down to its junction with Station Road. Turn left. The Metrolink sign indicates Crumpsall Station.

4. The Irk Valley and Heaton Park

This short walk is planned to take in a good part of Heaton Park, one of the finest areas of parkland in any northern city; but an interesting prelude is the little Irk Valley with its old industry and Crab village perched on the edge of Higher Blackley – and the old Pleasant Inn.

Distance: 4 miles (6km)

Maps: Landranger 109; Pathfinder 713.

Start: Bowker Vale (Metrolink)

Finish: Heaton Park (MetroLink)

Access: Metrolink – Bury line. Motorists should park at any station and take the Bury line train to Bowker Vale.

The Pub

The Pleasant Inn, Crab Village (Robinson's – CAMRA listed). At the edge of the huge Higher Blakely housing estate lies the 18th century village of Crab which still keeps something of its village character, most notably the well named Pleasant Inn, with its comfortable lounge and little snug. Robinson's Best bitter and Mild on tap, with Old Tom in the winter.

The Walk

From Bowker Vale station descend to the main Middleton Road. Cross with care, turning right uphill before taking the first road left Bowker Bank road, and then after 200 metres, take a track on the left which swings into the valley, under the railway bridge carrying the Metro, towards mill ponds in Bowker Vale below.

Before reaching the entrance gate into the old mill complex, look for a narrow, not very clear path on the right along a grassy bank through scattered birch trees. Follow this as it broadens and becomes more distinct, through the wood and along the mill-side above the old mill.

The path soon bears left down some steps – avoid a right turn into a
housing estate, but follow the path down through trees in front of the
mill, bearing right by the little River Irk – a tributary of the Irwell –
below as it flows out of the millponds. Then cross the river at a concrete
footbridge before continuing right along a riverside path downstream,
through pleasant open space until the path bears left up steps to join
Blackley New Road.

The Pleasant Inn, Crab village

Turn right. Follow the main road for a little over a quarter of a mile past
Ashenhurst Works on the right, and a long row of terraced houses on
the left beyond which is an area of scrub-land; between a derelict shop
and a second terrace is an opening to a short stretch of track which
ascends to the left where a clear concrete path, (not indicated on any
map), climbs the hillside, behind the first terrace before turning right up
hill with increasingly fine views. Keep on this narrow path which leads
all the way across the open space behind the housing estate, eventually
reaching a gap between houses into Sandyhill Road. Turn right here,
keeping right into Riverdale Road, then right again along Newry Walk,

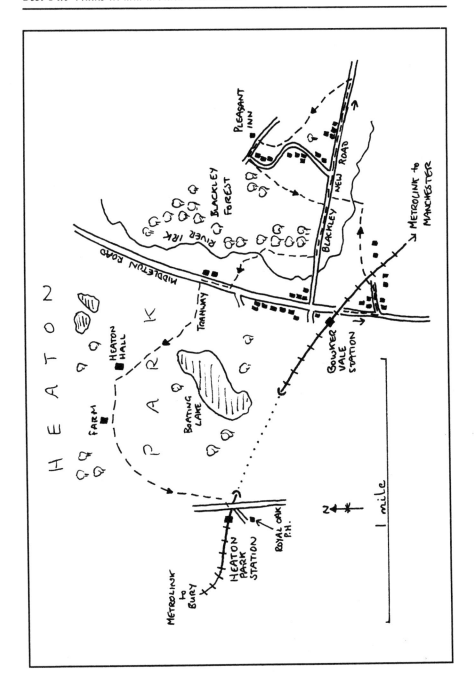

walking straight ahead across Printon Avenue into Selston Road into the broader Chapel Lane where about 60 metres on the right, on the corner of Crab Lane, is the Pleasant Inn.

To continue, walk back along Chapel Lane towards the wide entrance of Blakeley Cemetery, turning left by the Cemetery gates down Riverdale Road, but at the end of the Cemetery fence, look for steps on the right leading into a sadly neglected and rubbish littered area of open land. A rough path crosses this bit of wasteland towards the tall tower blocks ahead, the nearest being Blakeley Tower, where, among the rubbish, you will locate the start of a narrow green way on the right, fringed with trees, which soon becomes more distinct as it descends past a long vanished dye works into the valley to bring you back to Blackley New Road. Turn right here, past a small group of houses and cross the old mill dam, past the edge of a plantation of trees (Blakeley Forest) and more houses to a small car park which indicates the actual entrance into the Forest. Blakeley Forest is a lovely area of mixed woodland first planted by local Blakeley residents in 1953 as a part of Coronation celebrations and now a mature woodland covering the entire hillside above the Irk Valley. There is free public access.

Follow the main path straight ahead, but at each fork keep left along the distinct path, up steps, through the woodland, with yet another mill and mill pond down in the little valley on your left. At the top of a headland, keep left again, this time following steps down the other side, leading down to the River Irk in a pretty stretch of valley where, again not indicated on any map, there is a footbridge. Cross, but do not enter the avenue by the pedestrian gate ahead, but turn sharp right along a narrow grassy path which takes the public right of way up to Middleton Road, emerging in the forecourt of a garage by the Heaton Park Hotel. Turn right for 300 metres to cross Middleton Road at the safety of the pedestrian lights, to enter Heaton Park at its main southwestern entrance by the old tramway.

Heaton Park is over 600 acres in extent, and is one of the finest parks in Northern England; a magnificent area of formal gardens, informal wood-lands and grassland, with a boating lake, a great 18th century hall and tower, conservatories, a small farm zoo, and a museum tramway opera-ted by vintage Manchester trams – precursors of Metrolink. It was originally set out and landscaped in the 1770s by William Emes, a pupil of Capability Brown, with improvements added some 30 years later by

John Webb, a follower of Humphrey Repton. Heaton Park was acquired by the City of Manchester in 1902 when it was purchased from the 5th Earl of Wilton for £230,000 and has since developed to be one of the finest and most popular parks in the North of England.

Follow the main drive with the tramway, past the museum, keeping half right with the main drive past the playground and ascending gradually uphill towards the handsome neo-classical Hall set in formal gardens. The Hall with its fine colonnades was rebuilt in 1772 by the architects James, Samuel and Lewis Wyatt.

You may wish to spend some time exploring this magnificent park. Take the drive from the western side of the Hall, by the farm and road-train terminus, and keep left in front of the aviary before bearing right under the rustic archway towards the rose garden, a lovely romantic walk under tunnels, past grottoes and ornamental ponds; at a cross road of tracks, take the path through the woods half left which leads past the rose garden and walled gardens, soon joining the main path past cattle enclosures where Highland Cattle are usually to be seen, bearing left with the main track down to the entrance on Bury Old Road. Cross at the pedestrian lights to Heaton Park Metrolink Station.

5. Simister

The village of Simister keeps its rural flavour despite the massive conurbations on its doorstep. This walk from Heaton Park to Whitefield takes in the northern part of the Park, the village and explores some pleasant rural and urban paths between the motorways.

Distance: 5 miles (8km)

Maps: Landranger 109; Pathfinder 713

Start: Heaton Park Station (Metrolink)

Finish: Whitefield (Metrolink)

Access: Metrolink – Bury Line. Motorists should park at any station on Metrolink and take the Bury line train to Heaton Park.

The Pub

The Same Yet, Simister (Lees). This 18th century inn's curious name has a delightful history. Originally known as the Seven Stars, sometime last century, the pub landlord, in a hurry to get his faded sign repainted, hired a local signwriter who asked the landlord what he should write on the sign. Mine host, a little irritated with so obvious a question, simply said "Same Yet" meaning "Same Again". The painter took it literally and the words "Same Yet" duly appeared on the sign. As neither landlord or signwriter could agree to change the mistake, Same Yet has been the inn's name ever since.

It remains a typical local village pub, comfortable, but not too urbanised, the restaurant at the back hasn't changed the atmosphere, and there are impressive views across the Pennine hills. Nicely served Lees Mild and best Bitter, with excellent value bar food on offer most days.

From Heaton Park Station exit across Bury Old Road at the pedestrian lights into the park entrance, and follow the main drive as it curves between the Highland Cattle enclosures, descending by rhododendrons to the main drive to the Hall. Turn left up to the junction by the Hall, and right in front of the elegant facade of the Hall itself (For a fuller description of Heaton Park and Hall see Walk Four).

Classical Temple, Heaton Park

Continue past the Hall to the Orangery/Cafe, not far beyond which there is a narrow path which winds up to the beautiful – if sadly vandalised – classical temple on a low hillock, a magnificent viewpoint across the eastern edge of the park, surrounding urban and rural landscape across to the distant Pennine hills, the great Telecommunications Tower a prominent feature on the hill to the left.

Descend the opposite side of the Temple hillock, down the grassy slope by the rhododendrons where a faint path is visible, down to the tarmac path around its perimeter. Turn left along the path, winding past an old shelter to where, on the right, finger posts mark a short path into a large coach and car park, by tennis courts opposite the Telecom tower.

Bear right to the join the track at a pedestrian gate, leading into a broad enclosure, usually with ponies. At a fork, keep to the main track, left,

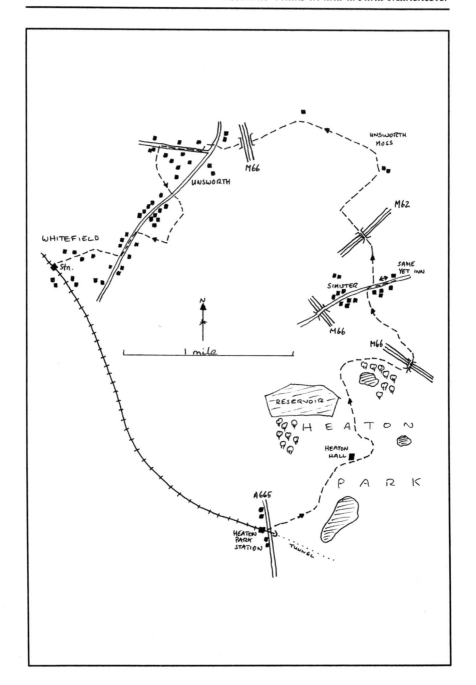

away from the trees, high above the golf courses and Fish Pond half concealed amid great banks of rhododendron.

Continue along the path as it curves right to the park wall and kissing gate. Turn right into the track which follows the wall for about quarter of a mile, gradually getting closer to the incessant roar of the M66 Middleton link motorway to a long footbridge which crosses the motorway.

Once across, turn left following an attractive old walled track which eventually reaches and zigzags past a row of attractive farm cottages known as Parkwood, continuing gently uphill along the now delightfully named Nut Lane to emerge in Simister Lane by the little chapel and school. Turn left through a village which isn't entirely suburbanised for some 250 metres to the Same Yet Inn.

Leaving the inn, retrace your steps along Simister Lane for some 150 metres to where a farm track, with a footpath sign, leads down to and across the M62 motorway. keep ahead with Egypt Farm to your left to a junction of tracks. Turn right here, following a long straight track parallel to the motorway to a group of farm buildings, Unsworth Moss. The path goes around the outside of the farm, keeping to the right (not to the bungalow) and, following the track, bears to the left along a tall hawthorn hedge, the way marked by not-always-easy-to-see rickety wooden stiles. Head for a small group of ramshackle old barns and buildings ahead, Moss Side (Moss is a typical Lancashire word for marshland – now drained) the path going behind and past these, still with the hedge to your right, stiles indicating the line of path.

The next bearing point is the farm and groups of barns known as Roe Barn. The path goes between Brick House Farm and Roe Barn, through a series of metal field-gates in the yard at Roe Barn. Keep the same direction – look for the waymarks – as the path crosses a stile in the hedge corner at the far side of the yard then follows a hedge and fence along the field edge to a further stile leading to a footbridge over a stream. Keep ahead now between soccer and rugby pitches, across the edge of a field and heading in a straight line to where there is a long tunnel underneath the M606 motorway.

You emerge into a tarmac drive behind the modern buildings of Castlebrook High School. Cross the main road, Parr Lane, to locate a short stretch of paved path between bungalows straight ahead. This crosses another estate road to emerge in Bloomfield Drive. Turn left to its junction with Sunny Bank Road.

Turn right here for 250 metres to where, past the Youth and Community Centre, there is an area of green, semi-wooded open space. A tarmac path, left, winds it way down this attractive little valley formed by the Parr Brook.

Keep left at the first junction (ignore the footbridge) to continue down the valley, but then fork right at the next junction to keep along the path downstream to emerge at an opening and remains of old farm buildings on Parr Lane. Cross and go right here for some 80 metres, but look for a narrow alleyway on the left between houses 241/243. This cuts through past gardens to the new estate road behind – keep ahead and slightly left to pick up its continuation between new houses. Follow the way left by gardens as it emerges in Calder Crescent, but after some 30 metres an opening on the right leads to a track behind the houses. To the right is a gate giving access to a recreation ground – Unsworth Football Club's home ground. Walk along the northern western edge of the playing field to a brick pillared gateway in the western corner. Don't follow the more obvious path left which just leads into an estate road, but turn right along a much narrower, if less obvious, ancient green path – known as Water Lane. This beautiful little path follows the backs of gardens until it arrives in busy Moss Lane.

After the delights of Water Lane, the last section of this walk is a slight anti-climax. Turn left along Moss Lane for 300 metres to the junction with Stanley Road, now serving as an entrance to an industrial and trading estate. Turn right here, and follow this rather urban road for about quarter of a mile, but to give a lighter touch at the end of the walk as the Metrolink sign at the junction comes into view, look for the narrow gate on the left which gives access into Whitefield's little park. Go through here, keeping straight ahead to the first junction where paths, right, lead past shrubbery and formal gardens to the entrance by the Metrolink Station; not quite Heaton Park, but a little bit of green to end the walk with. Beer lovers may well seek consolation in the fine red brick Church Inn on the corner of Bury New Road by the station with Holt's on offer.

6. Central Irwell Valley

Canals, Railways and long views of the West Pennines dominate this walk which takes in part of the Irwell Way in the Irwell Valley, looping around to enjoy views of Elton Reservoir.

Distance: 8 miles (13km)

Maps: Landranger 109; Pathfinders 712,713 and 700 (part).

Start: Besses o' th' Barn Station (Metrolink)

Finish: Bury Station (Metrolink)

Access: Metrolink – Bury Line. Motorists should park at any station on Metrolink and take the Bury line to Bess o' the Barn.

The Pubs

The Coach and Horses (Holt's – CAMRA listed). It's worth making the trip to Besses just for this pub. Only a hundred metres away from the roar of the M62 lies a living link with England's stage coaching history – the Coach and Horses, built in the 1830s in the heyday of stage coaching for the Manchester-Burnley coach just before the coming of the railways which were to dominate transport for more than a century. The pub still has its own stables, and an atmosphere which has changed little over the last 160 years; excellent Holt's Mild and Bitter on offer.

The Tap and Spile (Free House – CAMRA listed). Friendly pub recently themed in railway nostalgia style, with six real ales always on offer – recent brews excellently kept include Daleside, Thwaites, Marston's Pedigree.

The Walk

Besses o' the Barn might have a romantic old Lancashire name, but the Bess and her barn have long given way to featureless suburbs on the outskirts of Whitefield which are dominated by the M62 motorway.

The Bolton and Bury Canal, near Radcliffe

From the station exit, turn left into Bury Old Road to cross the motorway by the main road bridge, noticing the unusual box girder bridge on the left carrying Metrolink trams over the Motorway. About 100 yards ahead beyond the bridge, on the right, is the Coach and Horses.

But the walk actually starts at an enclosed footpath on the right, at the side of the motorway, which squeezes its way between motorway and a garage. Follow this between a wooden fence above the motorway embankment till it emerges in Stanley Avenue. Follow this round to the right into Cross Avenue, keeping ahead at the next bend to join Bury New Road by Junction 17 of the motorway interchange.

Cross the slip road via the refuge very carefully, heading towards the Mobil Garage on the corner. Head to the left and behind the garage and its "Minimart" where if you turn right, you'll find a stile leading into a narrow lane which squeezes between the motorway embankment and Prestwich Hospital.

This soon becomes a lovely wooded path descending into a little glade of willow trees, becoming a steep little gorge, the motorway and its noise

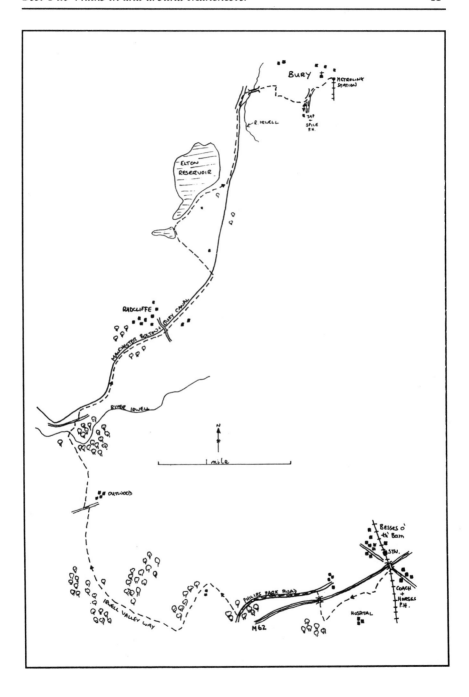

hidden by a bluff on the right. At the bottom of the clough, after about quarter of a mile, is a footbridge and a steep path winds its way up the hillside to the right, soon reaching a new footbridge across the motorway which leads into a cobbled lane, Phillips Park Road.

Turn left here and follow this lane as it climbs up hill, away from the motorway now in a cutting, soon passing the houses forming the edge of an estate. Keep ahead on the lane as it curves to the right passing a wood, but look for a narrow wooden stile on the right, about 100 metres past the bend, which leads to a narrow, enclosed grassy way along the hillside. Take this, as it bears slightly left. This continues past the edge of a little Jewish cemetery to emerge on a track, Old Hall Lane at the small synagogue that serves the burial ground. Turn right along this cindery track past Worsley Hill Farm, continuing for another 300 metres to a junction where Old Hall Lane bears away to the right.

Turn left here past the old buildings of Carter's Hill Farm, the path soon becoming a narrow grassy way which eventually emerges at a headland overlooking the Irwell Valley; the massive cooling towers of Agecroft Power Station dominating the view southwards, a mixture of industrial, urban and surprisingly rural countryside.

The path narrows to a way which winds by the edge of fields and rough grazing, curving down the hillside eventually to reach the old Clifton Junction to Bury railway line, closed in 1966. Take the second stile on the right which forms the footpath rather than the bridleway, and follow the old railway which takes advantage of a terrace above the Irwell Valley. Thickly wooded in places, where the line runs on an embankment there are fine views, and where it goes into a cutting – screening a large sewage farm – a feeling of intimacy. The line has recently been converted by Bury Council into a fine walking, cycling and horse-riding route carrying the Irwell Valley Way. Continue for just over a mile as the line curves northwards, and meets the A667 Farmworth-Whitefield Road near Outwood. Just before the bridge, the path climbs the embankment to a short stretch of track which leads to the main road. Cross the bridge, the path and the Irwell Way continuing on a signed path along a short road, Wood Street, by terraced cottages. Continue past the barrier along a track, noting the fine views of the West Pennine Moors with Peel Monument on the hilltop above Ramsbottom. The track follows the embankment above the old railway line, now in a deep cutting. At an electricity station, take the left fork, an attractive red shaley way by woods, past willows, down to the river where a steel bridge takes the path across the Irwell.

Turn right in the lane, but after 100 metres fork left at a beech hedge climbing uphill to the bridge over the canal, just before which a narrow, partly concealed opening leads onto the tow-path of the Manchester-Bolton and Bury Canal.

One of Britain's forgotten waterways, this canal, long since abandoned (though there is a preservation society) once served the mills and mines of the Irwell Valley until rail competition destroyed its economic viability. It now provides a lovely level footpath, a green sanctuary, with an occasional abandoned barge and lots of wildlife. It curves northwards past Scitson Fold Farm and into and through the centre of Radcliffe. Note the occasional old milestone, indicating 10 or more miles to Manchester.

Where the canal ends at a culvert, continue and cross the main road with care. Almost straight ahead by the canal-side is another serious real ale drinker's paradise, the Tut n' Shive offering bare boards, barrels of Boddington's, Thwaite's, Bateman's, Moorhouse's and other choice brews. If you decide to abandon the walk at this point or the beers prove too tempting, Radcliffe Station is a little less than half a mile along this road.

To the left of the pub is a gap back onto the canal. Easy walking now, soon leaving Radcliffe and heading along the disused canal under a disused railway bridge (interesting reflection of transport policies in Britain) through a surprisingly fine stretch of open country, the Metrolink line running close and parallel to the canal.

At the first farm bridge, leave the canal at the opening and walk up the track to Crow Trees Farm. The path goes to the right of the farm, and then becomes a beautiful, hidden path between tall hedges, climbing slowly towards the embankment of Withins Reservoir; as the path opens out and the grassy embankment comes into view, bear right down and over the footbridge and up to the edge of the reservoir. Keep ahead to a junction of tracks and turn right. This leads to the embankment of Elton Reservoir. Follow it to the right, again with fine views across to the outskirts of Bury and the West Pennine hills beyond.

Keep along the track as it bears away from the reservoir past a farm, crossing to pass a pub-turned-nightclub, bearing right to the canal bridge and sharp left back onto the tow-path.

Walk straight ahead now past the remains of Low Hinds Mill on the left. The canal suddenly dwindles away to extinction and you follow a track by its remains. Keep ahead into Wellington Road and the millscape of Bury, but where another abandoned railway crosses the road, turn sharp right to locate a concrete bridge which crosses the River Irwell. Continue along an enclosed path past houses to emerge on Bridge Road past houses, school buildings and the playing field of Bury Grammar School. Cross and turn right (the footbridge ahead over the railway is closed and in a dangerous state) for 100 metres past the football pitch to where a dirt track leads left past the workshops of the East Lancashire Railway at Buckley Wells, crossing the disused railway tracks to continue as Baron Street into Manchester Old Road.

Turn right and continue down Manchester Old Road where the third of three pubs – all worth visiting – is the Tap and Spile.

From the Tap and Spile, walk back up Manchester Old Road to its junction with Knowsley Street and the handsome ornamental clock-tower War Memorial. Almost opposite the Town Hall, cross to the tarmac path which starts by a curious slate-covered pyramid, and through a little park to the underpass. Turn right once through the underpass, then first left along the narrow path by a brick wall which leads directly to the Bury Interchange and the Metrolink Station.

7. Burrs and Summerseat

A walk to link Metrolink with the recently reopened East Lancashire Railway between Bury and Ramsbottom, taking in the remarkable industrial hamlet of Burrs — now a Country Park, Summerseat with Greater Manchester's smallest railway station and Nuttall Park.

Distance: 5 miles (8 km)

Maps: Landranger 109; Pathfinder 700, 701

Start: Bury Interchange (MetroLink)

Finish: Ramsbottom Station (East Lancashire Railway)

Access: MetroLink to Bury, return from Ramsbottom by East Lancashire Railway steam or vintage diesel trains (weekends only; for times from Ramsbottom ring 0161 764 7790) or frequent bus services from Bolton Road. Motorists should park at any Metrolink station and take the Bury line to Bury, or park at the East Lancashire Station Car park on Bolton Street to return by train.

The Pub

The Royal Oak (Thwaites – CAMRA listed) A really attractive Victorian pub whose recent renovation has kept its distinctive character and atmosphere, with central bar and separate rooms including a snug. Well kept Thwaites Mild, Bitter and Craftsman available – food Wednesdays to Sundays. Open all day from noon weekdays, Sundays usual times.

The Walk

From Bury Interchange walk past the bus stands with the Market on your right, keeping straight ahead past statues and shrubbery to the old Market Place. Turn left (with the East Lancashire Railway signs) along Bolton Street past the East Lancashire Railway's terminus, keeping ahead past the dark green tiled Snooker Hall before turning right into Castlecroft Road. This leads under the concrete viaduct of Peel Way, the northern by-pass. Once past the tunnel, turn left at the open area along Carlyle Street towards the river, passing an open field on the right, but,

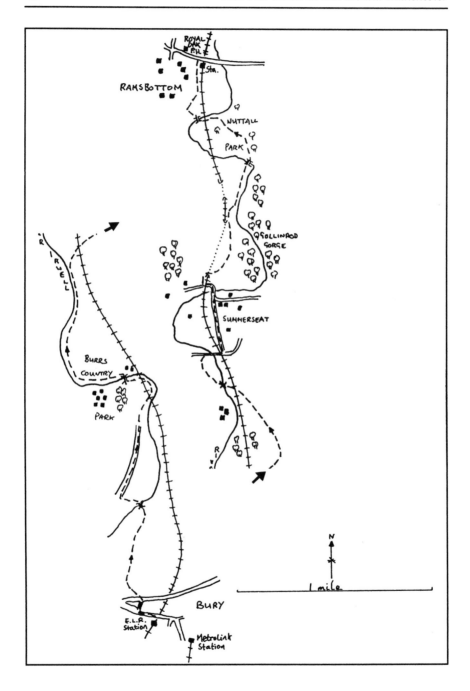

before reaching the factory at the riverside, look for a new-ish narrow gravel path on the right. Follow this by a grove of trees as it curves to the riverside, a delightful stretch past waterfalls to the old railway viaduct and weir ahead where as the path curves right, you see steps on the left leading up to a footpath which crosses the bridge.

Follow the path over the bridge to its junction with Woodhill Road. Turn right along this road past suburban housing until you reach the entrance into the new Burrs Country Park. Burrs is a fascinating industrial hamlet which grew up in the late 18th century around a water powered cotton spinning mill. The mill finally closed in 1933 but remains of the mill are being stabilised and interpreted as industrial heritage and the cottages restored as visitor facilities.

Make your way on the path through the complex of building foundations, forking right to go under the railway bridge carrying the ELR, and following the riverside around, back under the railway to the footbridge which leads to the Brown Cow, the oldest building in Burrs which began life as a farm in 1752.

Turn left at the Brown Cow, past the restored mill buildings including the water-wheel pit, and head towards the mill goit, the narrow canal carrying water from the river to the mill wheel. A path goes alongside the goit on a narrow embankment above the pretty river valley; follow it to the weir where the path follows the riverside. Fine views along the Irwell Valley are to be enjoyed from here, Peel Tower on Holcombe Moor a dominant landmark.

Follow the river for another quarter of a mile until the path leaves the river, crosses an embankment and joins a track leading under the railway and past Springside Farm. Follow the farm track uphill, but after 120 metres look for a stile on the left with the Irwell Way dragonfly waymark. This narrow path enclosed between fences follows the edges of the field before passing a small pond before descending alongside the railway where a stile on the left leads to a crossing of the railway line.

Cross carefully and join the lane. Almost directly ahead the lane crosses the river at a bridge. At the far side of this bridge a path on the right follows a grassy way through beech trees above the river. Follow this road until it emerges behind the gardens of a long row of cottages. Turn right in the track behind the cottages to emerge in the lane at Summerseat, keeping right under the bridge (watch for approaching traffic at this slightly dangerous corner) passing Summerseat Station (trains back to Bury), one of the loveliest little railway stations in the whole of Greater Manchester. Immediately past the station is a track on your left which runs parallel with the railway. Follow this keeping the same direction at a group of new cottages along the cobbled lane to join the road at Brooksbottom.

Turn left at the main road, walk back underneath the railway, past houses but turn right after about 50 metres at East View to head for steps which lead to a narrow cobbled path.

Follow this lovely old causeway as it ascends the hillside, soon passing the entrance to Brooksbottom Tunnel, following the line of the Tunnel to where it briefly emerges in a deep cutting before joining a track. Go right here, following the track down past shrubbery and the remains of old farm buildings to a footbridge over the river. Cross, the track now leading along the edge of Nuttall Park. Before reaching the stone buildings – Nuttall Hall Cottages – ahead, turn left past the car park into Nuttall Park.

Your route lies diagonally across the Park to its north western corner, head for the bowling green and turn left as you reach it – crossing to the riverside where a track goes under the railway and over the river to a junction by warehouses. Turn right for the station and the centre of Ramsbottom.

Ramsbottom – its name taken from Ransom or wild garlic rather than a male sheep – is an attractive, valley-side textile town which owed its prosperity to Robert Peel, father of the great Victorian Prime Minister, who in 1783 opened his calico printing works in the town. A more recent boost to the town's fortunes came in 1987 when the East Lancashire Railway, closed in 1972 was reopened as far as Ramsbottom for preserved steam and diesel trains, and as far as Rawtenstall in 1991. The ELR is now one of Britain's most successful preserved lines and it is worth doing this walk at a weekend if for no other reason than to travel the line. Extensions to Heywood are currently planned.

Turn left up Bridge Street, just past the station, and you'll find the Royal Oak on the right. Buses back to Bury Interchange (when trains aren't running) can be caught by turning left at the top of Bridge Street to the bus stop which is 80 metres on the left.

8. Along The Bridgewater Canal

A walk along the historic Bridgewater canal from Navigation Road to the Castlefield Canal Basin and Heritage Area then taking the recently restored Rochdale Canal under Manchester City Centre.

Distance: 10 miles (16km)

Maps: Landranger 109; Pathfinders 723, 724, 740.

Start: Navigation Road (Metrolink)

Finish: Manchester Piccadilly (Metrolink, Regional Railways)

Access: Metrolink – Altrincham line. Motorists should park at any station on Metrolink and take the Altrincham line to Navigation Road.

The Pub

Duke '92: A modern pub in a former Rochdale Canal warehouse stables building, cleverly converted to give an early 19th century feel, Duke '92 (named after the Duke of Bridgewater) has comfortable lounge type seating, Mozart on the stereo, yet retaining an atmosphere informal and friendly enough for canal ramblers not to feel out of place with city types. Beautifully kept Boddington's and superb food on offer, including a variety of Stilton and other French and English cheeses, patés and wholemeal bread in portions that even hungry walkers find difficult to finish – doggy bags provided.

The Walk

Leave Navigation Road Metrolink station and go down Navigation Road past the station car park and a recreation ground on the right, to a main road with a pub on each corner, 'The Navigation' on the left and 'The Old Packet House' on the right. Turn right over Altrincham Bridge and left into Halfords car park. On the right is a small Sea Cadet hut and alongside is a narrow path to the canal tow-path. Turn left onto the tow-path.

This is the pioneering Bridgewater Canal built by James Brindley for the Duke of Bridgewater to enable coal to be transported cheaply from the Duke's Worsley collieries to Manchester. In so doing the 'Duke's Cut' demonstrated the economic potential of canals, sparking a flurry of canal building all over the British Isles for the next half century. The Bridgewater Canal is important too, in that it is the first modern canal which was built as a waterway in its own right, rather than simply diverting an existing river as had previously been the case. During the course of the Bridgewater Canal's construction, Brindley had to solve every elementary problem of canal building. A system had to be designed for waterproofing the canal bed and the canal had to be engineered to cling to the contours of the land, using embankments, aqueducts and tunnels to maintain a level course.

The walk follows the tow-path along the canal with the Metrolink line as a constant companion for much of the walk. The canal itself is attractively lined with birch, brambles and interesting shrubs which have escaped from nearby gardens.

The tow path goes under two railway bridges and a little further on is a miniature railway on the left. Continue past a graveyard surrounded with a once elegant wrought iron fence, and then past Brooklands Station and under the brick Marsland Bridge. There are many old and new canal barges moored here, belonging to the members of the Sale Cruising Club. On the left is an elegant sandstone spired church.

Continue past Sale Station from where the Metrolink runs parallel to the canal, ensuring you are never far from the distant clatter of trams. Go past an old crane which would have once been used for loading canal barges and on past Dane Road Station with its elegant black and white tower. Then continue under Whites Bridge, to pass a huge gas storage tower, joining a short stretch of road before rejoining the tow-path to go under the M63 Motorway.

Continue past an attractive old canal building which is now a Club house. The surrounding countryside at this point, becomes increasingly built-up, with the canal acting as a green lung through industrial Manchester. Just past Stretford Station, the canal bends to the left and goes under another busy road to emerge at a canal junction and a small attractively landscaped area.

Go over the main bridge and then turn right, following the signpost to Manchester City Centre. On the right is an enormous Rail freight distribution centre, complete with the mechanism to load container shipments onto waiting trains.

The canal continues, threading its way along the backs of factories, passing the Manchester United football ground at Old Trafford. Continue along the canal until you reach an attractive metal footbridge, Throstle Nest Bridge, crossing over the canal. Go over the bridge, noting the mural depicting the history of Trafford on the wall behind, complete with a train and footballers, to join the tow path on the other side. To the right is a railway line and to the left the Manchester Ship Canal and Pomona Docks which has recently been landscaped and developed as an area of urban parkland for commercial and leisure development. Ahead there is a magnificent view of Manchester city centre with the Town Hall and G-Mex dominating the skyline.

Continue along the tow-path, passing some fine Victorian warehouses and crossing under the Metrolink line before emerging at the Castlefields Canal basin by Holme Junction lock where the Bridgewater Canal, Rochdale Canal and Manchester Ship Canal all meet, at the heart of Manchester's urban regeneration efforts. Walk round the edge of the Canal basin heading for the large imposing Castle Quay on the right hand side, which dates from the 1830s and was once known as the old Middle Warehouse. It has now been turned into flats and offices and the old canal arm which ran underneath the warehouse to allow barges to sail in to load and unload, has been reopened to make an attractive waterside feature.

Cross over the Dutch style metal drawbridge and continue alongside the canal to a metal footbridge by the Grocers Warehouse which was once the terminus of the Bridgewater Canal. Canal barges would enter the tunnels where the coal was then hauled up to the road above, by a crane powered by a water-wheel which has now been restored. Go up the metal stairs alongside the second metal drawbridge and turn left. Walk down a cobbled lane past a recently refurbished warehouse, Eastgate, into an open courtyard where on one side stands the Old Merchants Warehouse(1827), the oldest surviving example of a canal warehouse, and soon to be redeveloped, and the pub Duke '92, formerly the stables for the Merchants' warehouse.

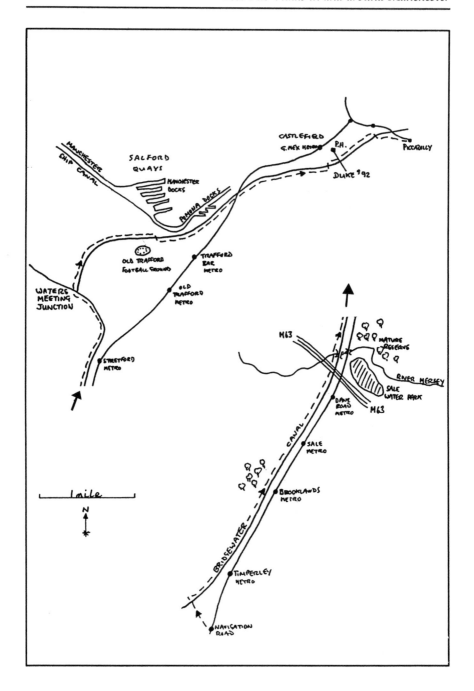

The Lock Keeper's cottage marks the start of the Rochdale Canal, built in 1805, linking Manchester with Sowerby Bridge in West Yorkshire. The cottage is designed to be at an angle to give the lock keeper a full view of the Canal Basin and ensure that tolls could be collected from those travelling on both the Rochdale and Bridgewater Canals.

It's a fascinating walk from here to the City Centre. You can still see where the canal was cut out of the red sandstone bed-rock by teams of navvies using little else but gun powder, picks and shovels. Follow the tow-path under a huge cast iron railway bridge, which is said to have destroyed the last remains of the Roman fort – hence the castellated towers on top which were meant to remind Mancunians of the city's Roman origins.

Continue under Deansgate tunnel and past a set of locks, note the lock keeper's cottage in the corner. A little further on the right hand side are some amazing mock Greco-Victorian pillars beside an American style Diner built on the old Albion Wharf. From here you can see the tower of the Refuge building, built of red brick and another Manchester landmark. The tow-path ends shortly afterwards, cross the road by the New Union pub and continue along the cobbled Canal Street. Note the lock keeper's house which straddles the canal itself. At the top of Canal street is the old Minshull Street Magistrates' Court, decorated with two carved dogs on either side of its doorway.

The canal tow-path re-emerges on the right hand side of the bridge. Continue along the canal to go through the undercroft which passes under Piccadilly itself, the experience made even more dramatic by the roar of water from the lock gates. The tow-path emerges at Dale Street. Turn left into Ducie Street and then right to Piccadilly Station. If you are walking this route unaccompanied, you may prefer to avoid the undercroft and in this case at Minshull Magistrates' Court, turn right and then first left and then right again along Ducie Street to emerge at the road leading up to Piccadilly Railway Station.

9. Dunham Town

A canal-side walk from industrial Timperley out into Manchester's Cheshire fringe, to Dunham Town, and an unspoiled estate village with post office, church and thatched cottages.

Distance: 4½ miles (7km)

Maps: Landranger 109; Pathfinder 740.

Start: Timperley Station (Metrolink)

Finish: Altrincham Station (Metrolink, Regional Railways)

Access: Metrolink; motorists should park at any Metrolink station to pick up an Altrincham train.

The Pubs

The Bay Malton, Oldfield Brow, is a large, free standing, rambling, red brick Edwardian pub, close to the canal and on the very edge of open countryside. Old style, yet very much a family pub, with a choice of food on offer, the beer is beautifully served Thwaites Dark Mild, Bitter and Coachman's.

The Orange Tree in Altrincham's Market Place (CAMRA listed) and handy for the railway station, dates from the 1880s and is one of the smallest pubs in Altrincham, a former winner of the local CAMRA pub of the year. Beers on offer include Courage Director's. Marston's Pedigree, Webster's Bitter and a regular guest beer – and all day opening.

The Walk

From Timperley Station exit turn right into the main Park Road, crossing the road (with care) and the canal bridge before taking the metal steps on the left of Nelson House, which look like an entrance to an office complex but actually lead down to the tow-path of the Bridgewater Canal.

The Old School, Dunham Town

Turn right along the tow-path, and follow the canal as it swings away westwards under railway viaducts and crossing roads through Broadheath, past offices, housing estates and gardens, playing fields, and a surprisingly large amount of industry both ancient and modern, with some large mills including the huge 1897 Linotype Works. Continue along the tow-path as industry gives way to new in-fill housing estates.

After just over two kilometres – about $1^1/_2$ miles – the conurbation begins to thin out as Greater Manchester yields to the more open landscapes of the Cheshire Plain. Where the countryside begins and Manchester ends, at the bridge carrying Seamons Road over the canal, take the exit path right up to the Bay Malton Inn. A gap in the fence to the left of the pub leads back onto the canal tow-path.

Suitably refreshed or restrained, continue along the tow-path as it winds through quiet farm-land, past quiet woodland, for another kilometre and a half to the next crossing bridge where an exit path leads to School Lane. Turn left here and walk through Dunham Town, despite its name no more than a delightfully unspoiled village which lies just within the Greater Manchester boundary – note the old school erected for the benefit of the township of Dunham Massey by one Thomas Wilson in

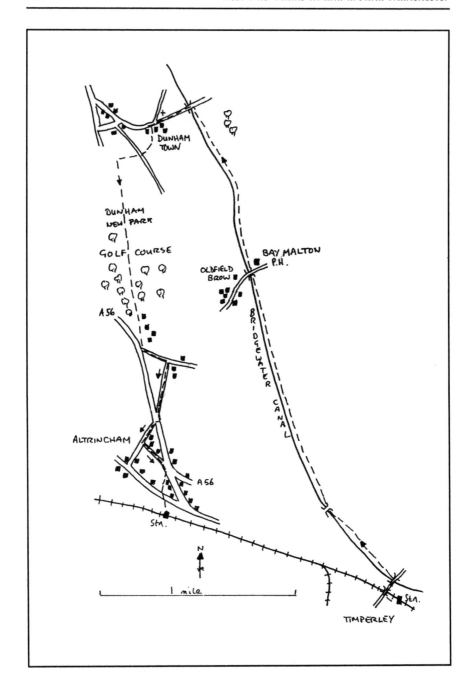

1759. There's also a handsome Victorian parish church, the Axe and Cleaver pub (Chef and Brewer), but look out for the thatched cottages on the left, set back along a track from the road.

Immediately past the road junction and village post office, take the narrow enclosed way on the left (signposted), but after 250 metres take the path right, over a stile and along the edge of a field until it meets Oldfield Lane. Cross this narrow lane before taking the path almost directly opposite which crosses another field to a T-junction of paths. Turn left here, the path crossing a couple of fields before emerging at the golf course at Dunham New Park.

Now this requires just a little care – the public right of way is directly ahead across the golf course and through the pine trees ahead. But many walkers will prefer to avoid treading the greens or being in the line of flying golf balls, and may wish to loop around the golfers' path to the right. If so be sure to return back to the line of path at the entrance to the pine woods, at a point directly opposite the stile that enters the golf course. This joins a broad track through pinewoods and rhododendron, past the little green-keepers' maintenance huts, keeping the same direction (avoiding two left forks) to join a rhododendron lined avenue which eventually becomes a lane leading into the busy A56 Dunham Road.

To avoid walking along this heavily trafficked stretch, turn sharp left at the corner where you emerge, down Highgate Road, taking the first turn right into Gorsey Lane, then bearing left at the first fork along the lower road, Booth Road, a quiet suburban road past some fine Victorian houses built by Altrincham gentry. Booth Road emerges after 300 metres back to the A56, but mercifully a footbridge avoids the need to risk one's life. Continue along Regent Road, turning second left down Market Street by the General Hospital, noting the fine 1873 Market House.

Altrincham blends the cosmopolitan nature of Manchester with the more rural feel of Cheshire – sophisticated, yet with an out-of-town feel. For 500 years a quiet market town on the edge of the Cheshire plain, in the 19th century it became a busy cotton weaving and engineering town linked to Manchester by canal and railway. Modern Altrincham is a shopping and cultural centre for South Manchester commuter country.

If you are heading for the Orange Tree, the Old Market Place lies directly ahead. The railway and Metro station are just along any road to your right.

10. Hale Moss and The Bollin Valley

From Altrincham to Hale via a medieval moat and manor house, turbary land, mature riverside woods ... and a glimpse of Manchester's ultra-modern airport.

Distance: 9 miles (14km)

Map: Landranger 109; Pathfinder 740, 741

Start: Altrincham Station (Metrolink)

Finish: Hale Station (Regional Railways)

Access: Altrincham Station is served both by Metrolink trams and by BR from Piccadilly via Stockport (Chester trains); Return- Hale Station has regular trains to Piccadilly via Altrincham (for Metrolink) and Stockport – NOTE: very poor Hale to Altrincham service on Sundays, afternoons only – for alternative bus services ring 0161 228 7811. Motorists should park at any Metrolink Station and take the Altrincham line.

The Pubs

Both Altrincham and Hale are well served with a variety of pubs. If you want a pint to start you on your way, try the **Old Mill** in Altrincham, about a couple of hundred yards into the walk. At the end there's the **Cheshire Midland**, a Sam Smith's house opposite Hale Station. The beauty of this walk, however, and best of all, is the splendid **Romper** at Ringway, about half way round the route and nestling at the very edge of Manchester Airport's vast cargo complex.

The Montgolfier brothers were probably making the first balloon flight when the Romper was opened about 250 years ago. Recorded in the 1800s as the "Romping Kitling" (a parody of the inn sign, a rampant Red Lion), the pub retains its rural charm despite the proximity of airport and motorway – the large beer garden is popular during the summer. Beams, flagged floors and open fires characterize both public and lounge bars and the wood panelled ceilings groan beneath the weight of a vast collection of water jugs. Connections with Ringway (the original name of Manchester Airport) are rife, with umpteen paintings and photographs of early passenger aircraft and second war bombers and fighters filling the walls. Airport trade, together with an excellent reputation for both beer and bar meals, ensures that this little gem is open all day on weekdays, with standard weekend hours. Beers on offer are Boddington's (it's a Boddies house), regular guests include Theakston's bitter and Cain's Formidable.

The Walk

Commencing from Altrincham station, turn right along Stamford New Road and walk to The Old Mill Inn. Cross the footbridge across the tramlines, turn right along Oakfield Road then bear left beside the telephone box along Oakfield Street. Continue ahead at the end, along the fenced path between the school and playing fields and cross the brook to reach the edge of a large area of municipal parkland.

Keep the railings surrounding the King George V Pond to your right and walk to the first corner. From here head half left across the neck of parkland to the stand of trees, beyond which a substantial tall white building is visible. Timperley "Old" Hall (now a restaurant) dates from about 1790 and stands beside the moat of the house it succeeded, the original Old Hall which was built in Elizabethan times by a member of the Arderne family, originating in Warwickshire but a leading family in northern Cheshire. An early member of the family was Mary Arden, mother of William Shakespeare.

Head back towards the railings around the pond and keep these on your right to arrive shortly at Timperley Brook. Turn left here and walk along the edge of the fairway, keeping close to the stream with a wary eye for possible golf balls. When you reach the wide, concrete tractor bridge across the brook (about 200 yards) cross this and follow the obvious track across the fairways, aiming just right of the white-painted old container at the far side.

This land formerly Hale Moss and Heath, now a golf course and cultivated farm-land dotted with ponds, spinneys and drainage ditches, was once vastly larger. Until little more than a century ago, it was largely an unimproved area of rough land, gorsey heath and fetid pools little changed since the last Ice Age. Nominally claimed by both the Earls of Stamford and the local people as common land, it stretched from the railway in the west to the motorway in the east, from Timperley in the

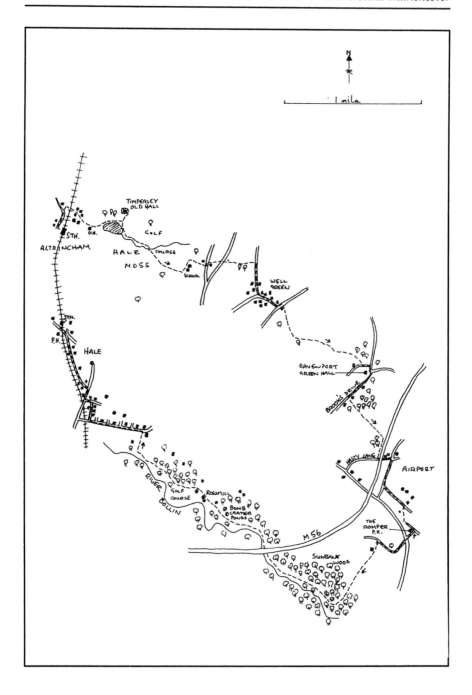

north down to the higher land to the south where Hale Barns now exists. Part of it was used as a race-course whilst there was a cockpit recorded near present day Stamford Park. Gorse and turf were cut by locals for use as fuel – the ancient right of turbary – a local baker swore by the quality of dried gorse as a fuel source for his ovens.

Over a period, the area became increasingly swampy, its stagnant pools a health risk both to humans and the animals they grazed there. Early attempts at drainage in the 1700s came to naught, the local gas company reclaimed a small area in 1847 and built one of the country's earliest gasworks there, but not until early this century was the Moss and Heath largely drained and reclaimed, partially by the Earls of Stamford (who provided Stamford Park in 1880 in lieu of grazing rights) and partially by the local councils.

Go through the gap-stile near the container and follow the field road beyond, and then left around, the school land. The track issues onto a minor road beside a modern thatched house. Turn left, cross the road and take the path on the right immediately beyond the garden centre. Cross straight over the main road at the far end, take the stile and walk ahead past the cattle shed. At the far end of the pasture, pass through the gap stile beside the rusted gate and continue to the end of the field, here turning right along the minor road.

Turn left along the main road at the end and left again where this road joins Clay Lane. Cross Clay Lane then turn right along the signposted footpath along the farm drive of Ash Farm. Pass by the stables and continue ahead, past the farmyard dump and boggy remains of the pond, keeping the hedge on your left. Remain on the "lane" between hedge and barbed wire fence to its far end, climb the stile here and bear half left at a tangent away from the stream.

This direction brings you to a narrow, slippery plank footbridge across a further brook; once you've successfully negotiated this and the two stiles beyond, pick up the line of hedge on your left. This hedge-side path eventually blends into a green lane, ignore footpath signs to right and left and simply follow the rough lane to its end, emerging onto a minor road opposite the beautiful half-timbered Davenport Green Hall. This is the oldest surviving secular building in the area; painstaking research by local antiquarians suggests that it may occupy part of the site of the "lost" village of Arletone, mentioned in Domesday Book but abandoned at or soon after the time of the Black Death (1348).

Turn left to Roaring Gate Lane, right along this and right again a few yards later at the sharp bend, picking up the rough road known as Brooks Drive. This Drive was built for Samuel Brooks, a wealthy Manchester banker, to link disparate parts of the vast family estates; it ran from Brooklands Station to Warburton Green, a carriage road "double-hedged, tree lined and eight yards wide" according to documents of the day. Opposite the first house you reach, an old cast iron milepost, dated 1863, can be spotted near the hydrant .

Just after the second house on the left, a public footpath sign directs you into a pasture. Pick up the line of hedge on the left and walk up to the distant motorway boundary fence. Turn right along this, pass between the fence and the spinney and walk ahead to Hasty Lane.

Go left along the underpass, continuing ahead at the far end past the gaggle of cottages to the main road, bearing right along this. A few hundred yards brings you to Avro Way, turn left along this (please note that at the time of writing [spring 1994] the underpass is closed while the motorway is being widened. Should you find it still closed, then instead turn right along Hasty Lane to reach Hale Road. Turn left along this, walk beneath the motorway and bear left with the cycle lane along Runger Lane. A hundred or so yards on the right is Avro Way, thence as directed). Cross to the right hand side and, virtually opposite the first building on the left (about 150 yards) search out the stile through the wood-rail fence, then head for the diagonally opposite corner. Once over the stile here, go left along the abandoned Wilmslow Old Road to reach The Romper and a welcome half-way break.

Leave the Romper along Sunbank Lane, between the side of the pub and the brick built chapel. This is Ringway Chapel, built for Lord Crewe in 1720 and a haven for the substantial number of Nonconformists and Dissenters who lived in the area. Now disused, it stands on the site of an Elizabethan chapel-of-ease. The Crewe family were major landowners locally; in the 1840s a family member promoted a railway line between Altrincham and Wilmslow which would have run close to the Romper, but sufficient financial backing was not forthcoming and the scheme collapsed.

A tricky footbridge on Hale Moss

Cross the busy main road and continue along Sunbank Lane. Once round the sharp right-hand bend, continue for two hundred yards to the farm road on the left and turn along it. Stay with the rough road past the farmhouse, barns and stagnant farmyard pond and continue to the end of it. Beyond here, keep the hedge on your right and walk towards the woodland ahead. In the last field change to the further side of the hedge via the small stile and continue to the woods, entering by the stile in the corner.

Sunbank Wood is amazingly rich in wild flowers, birds and animals. The path follows a circuit past small, deep old clay-pits and through mature woodland; keep an eye (or ear) out for owls, woodpeckers, jays, tree-creepers, kestrel, sparrow-hawk, foxes, badgers, squirrels, weasels and rabbits for example.

Almost immediately bear left at the fork and stay with the path along the edge of the clough, smothered in spring with vast swathes of ramson (wild garlic). Bear left at the next junction of paths and follow this wide path as it winds through the woodland, soon passing one of the deep ponds, off to your right. Ignore the left fork opposite the "Wheelchair Layby" and continue straight ahead along the greener path to the next fork. Here go left and drop gradually down the edge of another well-wooded clough to the footpath signpost at the edge of the wood-land.

Climb the stile and turn right towards Pigley Stairs Bridge, crossing brooks and stiles as necessary as you follow the River Bollin down-stream. The woodland edge overflows with wild flowers from early spring to autumn – herb robert, campion, ground ivy, speedwell, woundwort, bluebell and St John's Wort to name but a few.

Don't cross the footbridge but remain on this northern bank, picking up waymarkers for the Bollin Valley Way. Simply remain with the riverside path, in a quarter-mile or so passing beneath the busy M56 motorway. A further few hundred yards finds you at a barrier giving access to a meadow. Go through this barrier to find, on the left in about fifty yards, an interpretation board outlining some of the plants to be found in this rich hay meadow, through which the path crosses (take this path rather than the main one into the trees). One feature the board fails to mention are a few small, overgrown ponds off to your right. These are said to be the result of enemy action, bombs being jettisoned by a German bomber following an uncompleted raid on Manchester and Salford and exploding in the wooded peace of the Bollin Valley.

On reaching the wooden railing, rejoin the main path and climb gently uphill, following the blue arrow. Cross the rough pasture and trace the path across another brook, following the Valley Way to the surfaced road at Rossmill. Bear left along this towards Hale golf course. Nothing remains of the mill at Rossmill, recorded in medieval times as Rass Mill, by 1700 it had definitely disappeared, its name recalled by local houses and the narrow lane.

Pass by Rossmill Farm barn to reach the first white-painted house. Immediately beyond this a narrow path is signposted, left, for the Valley Way and Hale Golf Course. Wind around with this path to emerge at the edge of a fairway and walk alongside this beside the trees to a signpost for Ashley. Walk down the track here for fifty yards, then turn left at the footpath sign this side of the brook. Pass by the footbridge and stay with the main path through the spinney, ignoring any side paths, eventually joining the river again on your left – keep an eye out here for kingfishers and herons.

The path soon diverges away from the Bollin and skirts the base of a rough, grassy bank to arrive at some rusty old metal posts. Turn right here along the narrow path, lined initially by a few laurel bushes. At the far end, turn left along Bankhall Lane. The sixth road on the right, just before the railway bridge, is Nursery Avenue. At the far end of this turn left to the main road, then right along this (unless you would like a pint at the Bleeding Wolf, opposite). First left past the pub, beside the church, is Cecil Road which takes you directly back to Hale Station. If you find there is no suitable train back to Altrincham, a bus runs at least once an hour [more frequently Mon-Sat] via Hale Station to Altrincham Interchange.

11. Worsley Woods

Canals and railways feature prominently along this walk. The Bridgewater Canal and its Worsley Basin and the Tydesley Loop line are part of Manchester's earlier and later industrial history. Both now form beautiful green corridors to and through lovely Worsley Woods, a precious deciduous woodland which even the Trans-Pennine motorway hasn't yet quite destroyed.

Distance: 6½ miles (10km)

Maps: Landranger 109; Pathfinders 712, 723.

Start/Finish (circular): Patricroft Station (Regional Railways)

Access: Hourly train service from Manchester Victoria (Liverpool local service) weekdays only. Sundays catch bus 10,11,22,63,65 or 67 to Barton Lane. (Car park by church on Liverpool Road).

The Pubs

The Queens (Boddington's). A lovely old pub, full of character, built in 1828 and arguably Britain's first Railway pub being built at the same time as the Liverpool-Manchester Railway was being constructed. It used to be known as The Patricroft Tavern but changes its name to The Queens following a visit of Queen Victoria to Patricroft in 1857 – the Queen proceeding to Worsley old Hall by barge, despite one of her horses sadly falling into the canal. It escaped demolition thanks to CAMRA campaigning.

It's a cosy, friendly pub that has kept it original four room layout. There's excellent Boddington's Bitter and the less usual Boddington's Mild on draught. At the time of writing informal access can be found for the energetic off the Manchester-bound platform to the pub, otherwise the official way in is 50 metres along Green Lane beyond the railway bridge.

The Stanley Arms (Holts – CAMRA listed) on Liverpool Road, Patri-croft, is a firm favourite of Manchester pub-goers. A friendly, street corner pub whose interior has changed little since Edwardian times, this is what pubs should look like without any plastic or fake reproduction furniture. And here's what must be the cheapest pub beer in Britain – Holt's excellent Mild and Bitter at time of writing (Spring 1994) still under £1 per pint! It's open all day, (sandwiches available) making this a serious rival to The Queens as a super place to end a walk – allow fifteen minutes walk back to the train.

Britain's first Railway Pub? The Queen's Arms, Patricroft.

The Walk

If arriving by train descend the steps from the platform, go through the pedestrian gate, crossing the busy Green Lane and up the steps directly ahead between Victorian blue-brick walls, to an enclosed path parallel with the railway. This soon reaches and crosses the canal by a footbridge – immediately beyond this descend the steps but keep left down more steps to the canal-side road, and, under the bridge, join the tow-path through a pedestrian squeezer gate. Turn left along the tow-path.

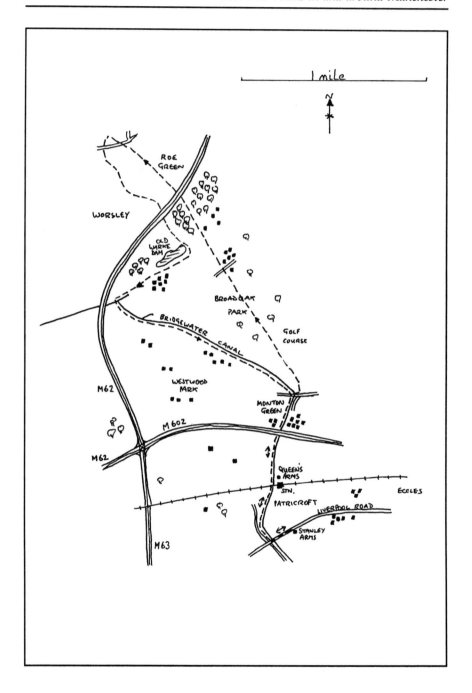

Walkers coming from the bus or car park at the traffic lights on Liverpool Road at Barton Lane/Worsley Road should follow Worsley Road northwards alongside the canal for around 60 metres to where the squeezer by the guard rail leads to a half hidden step onto the canal tow-path. Keep straight ahead to the railway bridge.

The Bridgewater Canal, opened in 1761 by the Duke of Bridgewater to link the extensive coal mines on his estate with central Manchester was built by the great canal engineer James Brindley. The canal, with its remarkable Barton Aqueduct over the River Mersey, is widely accepted to have played a major role in the development of Manchester's Industrial Revolution in the latter half of the 18th century. It is still a busy cruise and leisure waterway, its tow-path a popular walk. The distinctive reddish tinge of its water comes from iron leached from the old underground workings at Worsley.

Continue past an impressive red brick mill on the left, its embossed lettering announcing the Eccles Spinning and Manufacturing Co., before going under the M602 link motorway. From this point the canal-side opens out, with Monton church visible ahead. Immediately past the Bargee Inn, go through the pedestrian gate on the left leading up to the bridge that carries Parrin Lane over the canal. Cross with care and turn right towards Monton Green.

Monton Green overlooked by its handsome Victorian church is a delightful village green which has survived urbanisation as a much valued open space. Ignore the footpath sign (left) along Dukes Drive but keep ahead to pass the entrance of a small park, at the far side of which a narrow tarmac path leads from a railing, up by shrubs and flower beds to the top of what is an old railway embankment. Signs by the entrance gate indicate distances to Little Hulton and Ellenbrook.

This footpath, bridleway and cycleway is what remains of the old Tydeseley Loop, a freight and commuter passenger line that served the towns of Tydeseley and Leigh, an early victim of the Beeching axe in 1965.

It offers easy, high level walking, with fine views on either side across the golf courses of Broadoak Park, soon crossing Folly Brook, the old embankment now screened by sycamore, alder, birch, and elder trees.

Keep straight ahead for the next three kilometres, soon entering a long cutting and going through the tunnel under Worsley Road, just beyond which is the site of the old Worsley Station, its platforms now cosmetically restored as a picnic area. The loop line passes the edge of Worsley Woods, with several crossing paths, but keep ahead under the huge concrete tunnel and constant roar of traffic from the M62 Trans-Pennine Motorway; a contrast just beyond the tunnel is a little nature pond on the left.

When you reach a fork – the former junction – take the left fork signed Ellenbrook, under the left of twin bridges carrying Green Leach Lane over the railway. About 100 metres beyond this bridge, just past a footbridge over a stream, take the path which slopes up the embankment to the left which meets a crossing path at a stile. Turn left through a wooden gap stile into a narrow alleyway between a garden hedge and wall leading into Lumber Lane, the edge of Roe Green with its scattered Victorian cottages. Turn left to the end of the lane to its junction with Green Leach Lane; cross and almost immediately to the right two concrete finger posts lead into a track by woods. About 60 metres along here, to the left, a stile leads into the woods, along a muddy path which descends to stepping stones over a stream – Kempnough Brook – and steps. Follow the path to where it meets a broader track, signed FP Woodlands.

Keep on this main path for the next kilometre, ignoring crossing paths, keeping to the left of Kempnough Brook, going deep into the lovely mature woodlands of Worsley Woods – oak, beech, chestnut now dominating, though rhododendron is increasingly in evidence.

The path returns to the huge embankment of the Motorway, and stream and path go along a grim concrete canyon, a reminder of the devastation inflicted on Worsley Woods, one of the last unspoiled woodlands of west Manchester, when the Motorway was built. Plans to add further lanes – strongly resisted by local communities – threaten even more devastation.

Though it is a relief to emerge into the woodlands, the non-stop, deafening roar of traffic, which dominates the woods and this part of the walk, continuing as far as and beyond Worsley Basin, indicates another form of pollution of the environment resulting from our car and motorway culture.

At the gate by the black and white lodge, take the right hand, narrower track which leads past willows and wetland and eventually the waters of Old Worke Dam. The track goes past the dam and between iron railings to join Mill Brow by attractive cottages to emerge at Worsley Delph, an ancient flooded sandstone quarry where, as interpretation boards explain, tunnels led into no less than 52 miles of underground channels serving the Duke of Bridgewater's coal mines as far as Walkden and Farnworth.

Cross the Worsley Road to where, just by the telephone kiosk, steps lead down to a walkway which crosses the canal at a footbridge, past the half timbered Pack House to emerge on Barton Road. Cross, turning left over the canal bridge, at the far side of which, concealed, steps lead down to the canal tow-path. Turn right, back under the bridge, following the tow-path past the attractive canal basin, usually busy with houseboats, barges and leisure craft, past lawns and grassy verges, and then a long, easy stretch of canal, sadly more suburban in feel, with Monton Church a landmark once again ahead.

Keep ahead to rejoin and retrace steps beyond the Bargee Inn, Spinning Works and Railway, continuing for another 500 metres to where the canal goes under Liverpool Road – a half hidden step by the huge road sign leads to the sidewalk and Liverpool Road at the traffic lights.

Turn left along Liverpool Road for 200 metres just past the Spinners Arms to where, almost opposite, on the corner of Eliza Ann Street, you'll find the Stanley Arms. It really is worth the extra walk – though leave time also to call at The Queen's.

12. Canals Old and New

A cross country ramble from Altrincham to Partington on the edge of the
Cheshire plain and Mersey valley, through countryside which is both deeply
rural and yet with ample evidence of modern heavy industry.

Distance: 8 miles (13km)

Maps: Landranger 109. Pathfinder 723, 740.

Start: Altrincham Interchange

Finish: Moss Lane, Partington

Access: Metrolink, trains and buses from Manchester to Altrincham; regular
buses 247/8 run from Partington back to Altrincham Interchange, tel. 0161-228
7811 for current timetable – always check times before commencing this walk.
Motorists should park at Altrincham and return by bus.

The Pubs

The route of this walk passes by or close to several good pubs. **The
Swan with Two Nicks** in Little Bollington is the first, about a third of a
way into the walk. Several centuries old and with a good reputation for
food, it's a Whitbread house offering, amongst others, Boddington's,
Marston's Pedigree and Flower's bitter. Cheshire-brick built, the Swan is
an old farmhouse retaining open fires and heavy beams in the convivial
front bar area, hung with a vast selection of brass and copper, porcelain
figures and ornaments and a large collection of old bottles suspended
from the old beams. The larger back bar area is more of a dining area,
but there are also a few tables outside beside the quiet lane.

In Dunham Woodhouses, about half way through the walk, is the **Vine
Inn**, one of brewer's Samuel Smiths older pubs which retains its function
as the village local while catering for a busy lunchtime trade. There's a
pleasant beer garden.

The Walk

Turn left from Altrincham Interchange, then right at the crossroads, walking through the shopping precinct and up Shaws Road to the covered market hall. At the top of this turn left along Market Street, pass the hospital on your left and at the end turn right up Regent Road. This leads up to the main A56 Dunham Road. Turn left along this and continue the gradual climb up the ridge which marks the edge of the great mosslands for which this walk is destined. The grand Victorian and Edwardian mansions standing in secluded grounds mark this area as one favoured by bankers and industrialists made rich by the textile and engineering industries of Manchester.

Cross the busy road as soon as you can and continue up to the fairly sharp left-hand bend at which point Bradgate Road branches right. Also at this corner is an old white gate slumping between white gateposts. Immediately to the right of this a fingerpost for Dunham Town points the way through a gap stile and into the trees. Follow the main path (ignore the left fork) through this stand of mature woodland and continue along the rough road beyond, striking down through beech and birch trees in the midst of Dunham Forest golf course.

On reaching the corrugated iron sheds, bear left this side of them, then half right with the footpath sign, this one a National Trust one, and for Dunham Town only. The track leaves the trees and continues across fairways (beware of rogue golf balls) towards a cottage in the middle distance. A pause for breath at the far side of the fairways allows time to appreciate the fine views across the great flatness of the mosslands to the heights of the West Pennines and outlying hills above Skelmersdale and Wigan. Simply climb the stile here and continue along the field-side path to the cottages in the distance.

These cottages are at Dunham Town, one of several settlements which owe their existence almost entirely to the Egertons of Dunham Massey, the major landowners in the vicinity. As you reach the road, turn half-right (not along the narrow road, sharp right) and walk to the junction marked by the ancient tree standing comfortably amidst old cottages and farmhouses. Turn left along Woodhouse Lane and walk to its end at the main road. Turn right (still Woodhouse Lane) then climb the ladder stile beside the white gate on your left, here entering the estate surrounding Dunham Massey House.

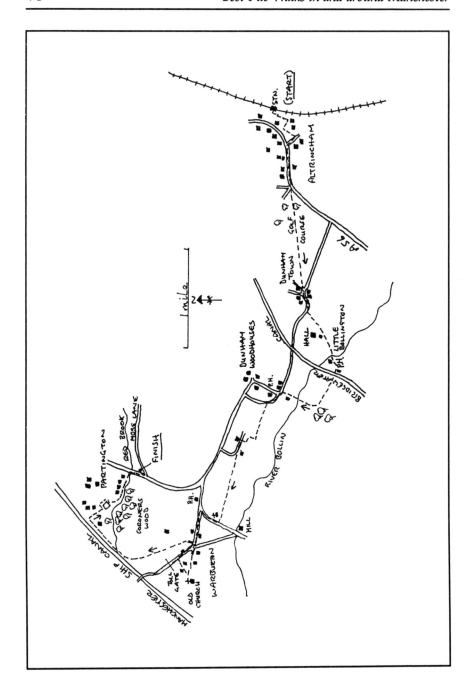

Broad avenues and carriageways lined by majestic beech, oak and chestnut radiate from the Hall, an eighteenth century building on the site of a medieval manor, home to the Earls of Stamford and their ancestors as recently as 1976 when the National Trust assumed responsibility. The House, containing a renowned collection of period furniture, paintings and silverware, is open daily except Fridays, approximately from Easter to early November. The hundreds of acres of parkland is open year-round and is grazed by a large head of remarkably tame fallow deer, including rare white ones. Near to the House and stables block is the ancient estate water mill, fully operative and occasionally open for viewing.

The walk leaves the estate via the ladder stile below the mill, heading straight across low lying pastures to the tower of another mill, this one a Georgian flour mill at Little Bollington, now converted into luxury apartments. A few steps beyond the narrow metal footbridge is The Swan with Two Nicks, a name harking back to the practice of Swan-Upping whereupon swans "owned" by the Vintners Company (originally an ancient guild) were identified by two nicks being made in the beak of every appropriate bird. More detail appears on the pub's printed menus.

At the tiny green a few yards beyond the pub, bear right along the cobbled roadway and walk beneath the aqueduct. This carries the Bridgewater Canal, the first canal of the post-Roman era in Britain, built in the 1760s for the Egerton family largely by that renowned engineer James Brindley. Take a few minutes to scramble up onto the aqueduct to appreciate the massive feat of engineering involved in the building of the aqueducts and embankment.

Back on the cobbled road, walk the few yards to climb the stile beside the gate and then the few yards further to two stiles. Climb the farthest, right hand one and bear half right, tracing the field road to the copse. Beyond this skirt the field edge, left, to a further stile, once over which turn sharp right and walk to the stile beside the wooden pylon. You're now virtually down on the mosslands but still high enough to gain views across to the Dark Peak, the West Pennine moors above Bury, Winter Hill and its TV transmitter above Bolton and, further west, the lower ridges of Ashursts Beacon and Harcles Hill on the mid-Lancashire ridge above Wigan and Skelmersdale. Nearby, the slender metal chimney belching flame is at Carrington petrochemical works.

From the pylon drop down to and cross the footbridge, and follow the line of wires to the bridge over the river Bollin, then stay with the farm road to reach cottages in Dunham Woodhouses, another estate village remodelled in the 1800s on medieval foundations. Turn left, then at the sharp bend go ahead along Barns Lane; the entrance to the Vine Inn is just up Station Road (right at the bend).

Wind along with the tree-shaded Barns Lane and past the farm to reach a footpath sign on your left for Warburton. The path, often no more than an uncultivated strip above crops or ploughed furrows, traces the edge of several fields. An excellent appreciation of the whole area of former mossland (drained and reclaimed in stages from around 1700) is gained here, miles of oak, willow and alder-lined drainage ditches delineating large fields, clusters of cottages and old farmhouses favouring slightly higher mounds and copses of trees feathering the horizons.

Waymarks indicate the way around the fields to a gated crossing over the old goods line, "Beware of Trains" signs now referring only to ghost trains, the track having been removed a few years ago. Cross the old line and continue along the slight embankment across the field, then follow the waymark arrows left, then right up to the minor road, turning left along this.

At the sharp bend go ahead along the "No Through Road" and, in fifty or so yards, bear right at the corner along the rough lane, the direction of the sign for Warburton is slightly misleading. Cross the overgrown stile beside the gate and continue ahead, crossing a further stile and small footbridge. Within yards change to the further side of the old hedge and continue westwards. In the distance is the great viaduct at Thelwall, carrying the M6 motorway high above the Mersey and the Manchester Ship Canal. Nearer to hand, the buildings off to your left are those at Heatley Mill beside the Bollin, a site used for a thousand years and more but now derelict.

Go straight across the sunken field roadway and at the main road turn right, pass by the Victorian St Werburghs Church and continue to the sharp bend. To the right is the Saracens Head Inn (Greenall Whitley beers – Walkers, Davenports, Stones), one of a number in the area to claim association with the outlaw Dick Turpin who supposedly took refuge in the area when on the run – in his day the mosslands were still largely heath, fetid pools and swampland crossed only by a few tracks and causeways. The route of the walk at this bend is left along Paddock Lane which you follow to its end, whereupon go straight across Townfield Lane and along Wigsey Lane. Notice at the junction the base of the ancient village cross and the stocks, partially restored in 1900.

This is the heart of Warburton village, Wigsey Lane, unusually for this area, lined by sandstone slab vaccary fencing. Bear left at Church Green to find the old church of St Werburgh, now essentially disused and in the charge of the Redundant Churches Fund (whose London address is "St Andrew by the Wardrobe"). It's of Saxon origin, the current building a mixture of twelfth century timber-frame, seventeenth century sandstone and eighteenth century brick. Warburton itself was possibly a Saxon stronghold (Werberghtune, the "bergh" element meaning fortified site) developed at the site of sandstone quarries dug by the Romans to provide stone for the building of their fort at Manchester. Later, a priory was established by the Premonstratensian "White" Monks from their English Mother House at Glasson, near Lancaster.

Return the few yards to Church Green and go ahead along the rough track between cottages. Those on the left, with latticed windows, were created from one of the village pubs, the Pipe and Punch-bowl, recorded as closed as long ago as 1851. On reaching the road, divert left for a few yards to the toll gate. This, still working, guards a crossing of the River Mersey, a bridge being built in 1863 to replace a ferry. This in turn was superseded in 1894 by a high level bridge across the new Manchester Ship Canal. Walk a few yards beyond the toll booth to find the rusting metal balustrade of the old bridge, crossing no more now than a few pools and a crop-rich valley – the old course of the Mersey.

Return to the toll gate and fall back to the village stocks. Turn left along Paddock Lane, then left again a few paces later along Park Road, in about 150 yards bearing slightly left along the rougher roadway, signposted for Partington and surfaced by rounded cobble-stones. Park Road, which you leave at this point, derives its name from the old manor house and parkland at the centre of medieval Warburton. The moated manor had disappeared before the Civil War, its site later partially built over by Park Farm about 170 years ago – the large brick building and substantial barns off to your right in the midst of pastureland and a stand of trees. The family seat was moved to Arley, some miles to the south, although no reason for this has been forwarded.

The cobble-stoned track follows the edge of what was the course of the Mersey; this becomes apparent as the Ship Canal comes into view, with the course of the Mersey visible beneath a small outcrop of sandstone, while the new canal cut, passing beneath the bridge, broached virgin territory. For much of its upper reaches the Ship Canal follows the natural course of the rivers Irwell and Mersey. These had been made navigable between 1721 and 1734, but suffered badly from silting and variable water supply. Completed in 1894, the new Canal linked Manchester and Salford with deep-water channels in the Mersey estuary, so that ships up to 15,000 tons were able to use the 36 mile waterway. Immensely busy until the 1970s (Manchester was one of Britain's top five ports), few ships now use these upper reaches, generally only visiting warships, tankers and refuse barges for example.

Remain with the path above the Canal, soon crossing over the Red Brook as it joins the cut and, a little way further along, passing an isolated house. The ruins next to this are probably associated with a small steel mill which was built about a century ago and took advantage of the new transport medium. On the opposite bank of the Canal, the Glaze Brook tumbles beneath the spans of abandoned bridges which once carried the Ship Canal Railway system.

Stay with the path and pass through the green gates, a modern housing estate now just ahead at the near end of Lock Lane, its name recalling the site of one of the original locks on the Mersey and Irwell Navigation. One historic feature with origins in medieval times – and which closed down only in 1992 – was the passenger ferry across the Mersey Ship Canal; Bob's Lane Ferry plied between the far bank in Cadishead and Lock Lane, the last of half a dozen or so such facilities on this stretch of the Canal.

The way is right immediately past the green gates, along the narrow tarmaced roadway to the treatment works at the end. Bear left just before these through the gap stile and into the long pasture or recreation ground. Keep to the right-hand edge to reach another gap stile beside black metal gates a little way beyond the grounds of the works. Go through this and walk ahead along any of the tracks into the area of woodland. This is Coroners Wood, said to be a place of burial used by the monks of Warburton in medieval times and one of the oldest wooded areas in the County.

Work your way to the stream, Red Brook, and turn upstream, following the well used path between the brook and an encroaching housing estate to reach a bridge carrying the main Partington to Warrington road, about half a mile distant. Join the road, turn right across the bridge and walk gradually uphill to the bus stop on your left, at the junction of the main road and Moss Lane. Buses from here follow a remarkably rural route back across Carrington Moss, past centuries-old farms and cottages to Altrincham.

13. Pennington and The Wigan Flashes

Water dominates this walk between Leigh and Wigan, not only the Leigh branch of the Leeds-Liverpool Canal, but the astonishing artificial "Flashes" of Pennington and Wigan which are such a wetland landscape feature and haven of wildlife.

Distance: 9 miles (15km)

Maps: Landranger 108, 109; Pathfinder 711, 712, 723

Start: Leigh Bus Station

Finish: Wigan

Access: Leigh is served by a variety of buses from Manchester's Arndale Centre, including Service 34 which runs every 30 minutes (not Sundays) and takes 47 minutes. Service 35 takes just over an hour and operates every 30 minutes weekdays, hourly Sundays. Frequent return trains services from Wigan Wallgate Station to Manchester. Motorists should park in Wigan and take bus 593 to Leigh. Full details from GMPTE hotline on 0161 228 7811.

The Pub

The Swan and Railway (CAMRA listed) in Wigan's Wallgate, just two minutes from the station, is a lovely Edwardian building filled with railway memorabilia and pictures of swans. A magnificent stained glass window over the bar depicts a Lohengrin-like swan accompanied by two American style steam locos complete with spark arresters. Beer includes Banks Mild and Bitter, Bass, Courage Director's and regular guest beers.

The Walk

From Leigh bus station turn left to the main road, crossing the main A572 at the pedestrian crossing, turning right to the traffic lights and main road junction by the Eagle and Child, then left along the A579 to the canal bridge, going over the canal bridge then turning sharp left before the Bridge Inn onto the canal tow-path. Turn left along the tow-path and walk back under the road bridge, continuing past converted warehouses and new buildings in old warehouse style, soon clearing the suburbs, the canal following an elevated way along a broad embankment above a low lying golf course, marshy ponds and scattered woods soon coming into view.

Pennington Flash

This is the Leigh Branch of the Leeds-Liverpool Canal, and interestingly enough was the last section of the canal to remain in commercial use, still carrying coal to a local power station as late as the 1970s.

After a little over half a mile along the canal, as the canal swings northwards, look for a set of steps cut into the steep side of the canal embankment.

This leads across and down into the woodland. Follow the path straight ahead which leads between pools and follows the side of a stream at the edge of the golf course. At a junction of paths keep right to follow the

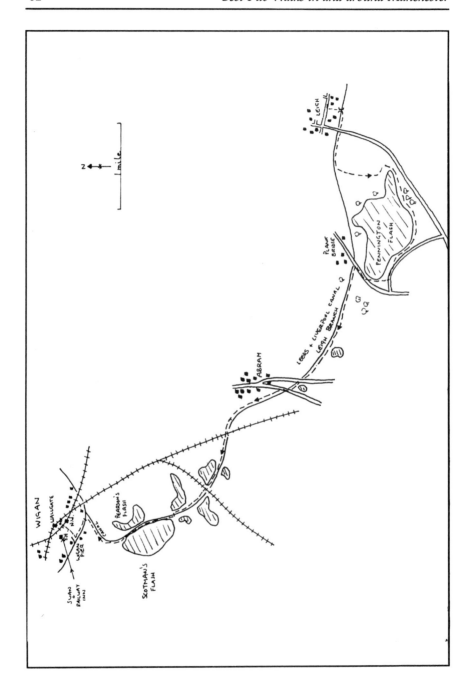

edge of a spinney and open grassland, curving past picnic tables at the side of Pennington Flash. Keep ahead for the car park, small visitor centre, golf shop and, usually, a refreshment van. There are public toilets in the golf course club house.

Pennington Flash is now a delightful country park and nature reserve. It wasn't always so. A "Flash" is a pond created by mining subsidence as old worked-out seams have collapsed. A quarter of a century ago this was an area of dereliction – coal tips, refuse dumps and debris. It is now a wonderful wildlife sanctuary, especially noted for its bird-life – both native and migrant species. Birds regularly to be seen include Canada geese, mallard, redshank, ringed and little ringed plover, common sandpipers, heron, oystercatcher, gulls, turnstones, dunlin, teal, great crested grebe, ruddy duck, goldeneye and short-eared owl. If you have a dog with you, please ensure that it is on a lead through the Reserves, especially at nesting time.

Follow the path by the edge of the car park and keep right over the little footbridge at the far end which crosses Pennington Brook which drains the lake. A choice of paths, but most people will prefer to keep right along the narrow path which follows the lake-side edge through attractive scrub woodland, rich, in spring and summer, in wild flowers – foxgloves, toadflax, potentilla, wood sage, cornflower, vetch, teasels, bullrushes are amongst many to be enjoyed – and are a haven for butterflies in the summer.

Keep to the lake-side path past frequent bird hides; where one path reaches a dead-end, the lake-side route is actually on a left fork leading away from the lake behind trees. This path bears right and goes through a couple of stiles and into Sorrowcroft Farm. Go straight through the farmyard, past ponds and Leigh Sailing Club's moorings, and along a track by cottages to join the main road.

Cross and turn right here, following the road round a sharp bend left to where 200 metres past the bend a signed path leads on the right down the drive of Mossley Hall. The footpath goes to the right of the Hall and follows the edge of a couple of fields by a ditch to emerge on the road at the northwestern tip of Pennington Flash. Bear right to join the road and follow it past signs of old workings still in the process of being re-naturalised to the curious little swing bridge over the canal – Plank Lane Bridge.

Turn left along the tow-path.

For the rest of this walk directions are hardly necessary – four miles of level tow-path, but interesting walking because of the elevated nature of the canal with long views across the Lancashire and Cheshire plain ahead – though if there is a head-wind, going can be surprisingly tough in this very exposed area with nothing much between you and the Irish Sea to break the force of the wind. You soon pass Garrard's Bridge carrying a disused railway trackbed, then as the canal turns northwards Aye Bridge (with an inn) near Dover and, after around two miles the A58 is reached where the tow-path changes sides to the east bank. Soon follows the West Coast main line railway at Bamurlough whose flashing electric trains will have been animating the horizon for some time. Just past an area of derelict line lies Ince Moss, the first of the artificial lakes that forms the Wigan Flashes. Beyond the next railway line this time carrying the railway from Liverpool and St Helens, the canal enters an even more remarkable Lakeland landscape, and beyond a spoil heap, water at both sides of the canal's embankments. As at Pennington, this old industrial landscape is slowly recovering and renaturing, scrub woodland as well as water providing a remarkable habitat for wildlife.

These are the Wigan Flashes, again artificial areas of flooding caused by the subsidence from the extensive coal mines that, during last century, created the wealth on which Wigan's prosperity was based. Just before Pearson's Flash (on the right) and Scotsman's Flash on the right, the canal tow-path again changes sides to the west bank. At this point there is water all around you but on three different levels.

The tow-path curves to the right at Poolstock to parallel the B5238 into Wigan. At the junction with the main Leeds Liverpool canal, keep right with the tow-path to the bridge carrying the B5238 where you exit from the canal and cross the bridge to regain the tow-path at the far side, entering that fascinating area of industrial heritage, museum and theme park known as Wigan Pier. The Pier itself is no more than a modest coal staithe, made famous by George's Orwell polemical Road to Wigan Pier describing the poverty of 1930s working class life. The complex of old mill buildings, linked by tow-path and waterbus are now one of the top tourist attractions of the Northwest. Highlights include Trencherfield Mill with its mighty steam powered mill engine and the "Way We Were" exhibition of Wigan's social history.

Directly ahead, you'll see The Orwell pub, named after the writer who, ironically perhaps, put Wigan on the literary map. Cross the footbridge (the Orwell has a good reputation for its real ale but isn't really a walkers' pub) to the exit onto Wallgate. Cross the road with care and turn right up to The Swan and Railway on the left, opposite North Western Station; Wallgate Station is another 100 metres up Wallgate on the left.

14. Haigh Country Park and Lady Mab's Walk

This walk from Blackrod to Wigan crosses Haigh Country Park, a spectacularly beautiful woodland park, the route closely reflecting a sad medieval tale whilst exploring a green walkway leading to the centre of Wigan.

Distance: 6 miles (11km)

Maps: Landranger 108, 109; Pathfinder 700, 711, 712,

Start: Blackrod Station

Finish: Wigan

Access: Frequent rail service to Blackrod from Manchester Piccadilly and Oxford Road (Blackpool service) via Salford Crescent and Bolton, returning from Wigan Wallgate. Day Ranger tickets save costs. Motorists should park in Bolton and catch the train to Blackrod, returning from Wigan to Bolton. Winter Sundays when there is no service to Blackrod take the 575, 617 or 840 bus from Bolton Interchange.

The Pub

The Millstone (Thwaites – CAMRA listed). Extremely pleasant town local, friendly, comfortable, with excellent Thwaites bitter and mild. Closes between 4pm and 7.30pm – food available daily.

The Walk

When Sir William Bradshaigh, Lord of Haigh, went on Crusade to the Far East in 1314 and disappeared for seven long years, his wife, Lady Mabel gave him up for dead and was persuaded to marry a Welsh knight. But her husband returned, slew the interloper and the unfortunate Lady Mabel, in days before feminist values, was forced to do a weekly penance for the rest of her life by walking barefoot in sackcloth and with a candle, from Haigh Hall to a wayside cross on the outskirts of Wigan. This walk retraces Lady Mabel's footsteps – though readers of

Mab's Cross

this guide are unlikely to walk barefoot and can enjoy a pint of excellent Thwaites instead of doing penance.

From Blackrod Station take the footpath which starts from the Preston end of the northbound platform – a cobbled path which leads between fields up to the main A6 road. Cross the road and go through the kissing gate straight ahead, the path continuing this time up cobbled steps which bear right and lead up to Castlecroft Avenue and into the main Manchester Road (B5408) in Blackrod.

Turn right past a group of attractive cottages for 100 metres to where Vicarage Road bears off left, keeping straight ahead along Greenbarn Road past the Community Centre at the far side of the car park from which a footpath (signed) leads between houses. Follow this path to the right behind gardens, through a stile, and continue along the edge of a field, still behind gardens, to a gateway with two stiles. Your way is over the wooden stile on the left. This path follows a hedge along the edge of a field, curving southwards for about three hundred metres to a gateway with a stile. Your path is to the right here, again alongside a hedge but where the hedge ends, keep in the same direction down a shallow valley. Continue to the next stile in the hedge ahead, crossing the stream at a little footbridge and ascending the other side. Make for the buildings of Freezeland Farm ahead – follow the fence to find a stile and gate to the left of the farm.

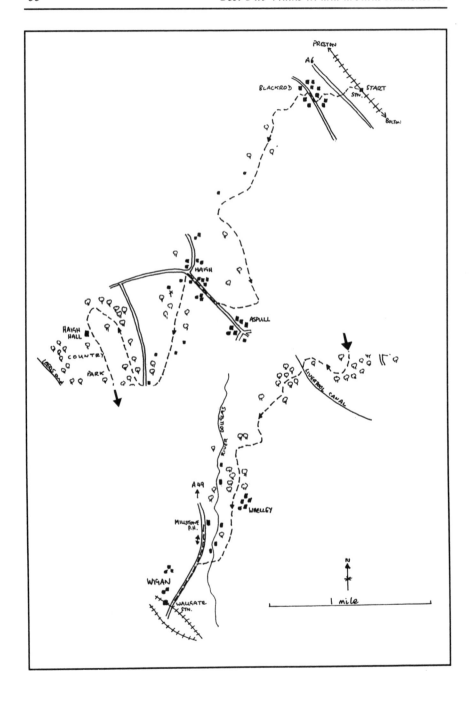

Turn right along the track in front of the farm cottage and follow the track as it climbs uphill, eventually bearing to the right. Where it curves back to the left, look for a stile on the left accessing a narrow path over the hill summit. Take this path, which joins a bridleway at the far side of the hillock. Turn left here to walk down a beautiful green track with superb views over to the south and west, across to Horwich, Rivington and Winter Hill and the outskirts of Bolton.

The track broadens to a farm track at the exit to Gorzens Farm, and enters Stanley Nook by its old village green. Turn right along Stanley Road past the New Inn (Burtonwood). Where Stanley Road joins the main road through Haigh, keep right along the cobbled way past the green.

Continue to Haigh Cross roads where there are no less than three pubs. From here, the route is a bridleway which leaves the cross roads at an ancient stone which marks the Boundary of the Hundreds of Salford. The track passes the side of the Parish church with views of the Haigh Windmill across the graveyard. Where the track to the cemetery bears off to the right, the bridleway continues straight ahead as a beautiful green way through a tunnel arch of trees.

The bridleway emerges at a disused railway line and cottages with a walled garden and a junction with a lane. Turn right. Almost directly opposite is a pedestrian entrance over a stile into Haigh Country Park.

Walk directly ahead crossing the miniature railway tracks, but at a junction of paths turn right through the park heading northwards to the Hall, gardens and the Stable Block where you'll find an excellent cafeteria, well stocked information centre, toilets, and exhibition areas.

The 260 acres of Haigh Country Park form one of the Britain's most popular country parks, with 40 miles of woodland walks, a little zoo, and a golf course. The Hall itself was built by the Earls of Crawford and Balcarres from wealth earned by the mining of rich deposits of cannel – a high quality, smokeless form of coal – on their land and in developing their own iron works on the estate. Now owned by Wigan Borough Council, the Hall is used for a variety of private functions and receptions.

From the entrance to the Stable Block turn left to Haigh Hall itself, following the main drive that leads from the Hall through the woods.

Keep along the main drives as it curves to the right through glorious mature beech woods, descending into the Douglas Valley soon crossing the Leeds Liverpool Canal in a lovely woodland glade, continuing through Lower Haigh Plantation to cross the disused mineral line from Ince, the drive again swinging round in a great curve as it follows a little side valley into the main Douglas valley.

About 80 metres before the drive crosses a handsome iron and stone footbridge over the Douglas to the Park entrance, look for a narrower path on the left which descends steps to a footbridge. Take this, climbing steps to the other side to join a path which goes down the wooded valley towards the centre of Wigan. Keep straight ahead as paths join from other directions, still with the river on your right, as the path becomes an urban way, eventually going underneath the massive concrete tunnel formed by Central Park Way inner relief road, past Central Park itself, Wigan's Rugby League ground, sacred territory for Rugby League fans.

The path terminates in Powell Street and the end of Central Park Way in the roar of traffic. Turn right for about 200 metres to the cross roads where Standishgate crosses Powell Street. Turn right again into Standishgate for a further 200 metres, past the school to where you'll see, by the roadside, the weather-beaten Mab's Cross where poor Lady Mabel made her weekly pilgrimage. She now lies reunited with her (first) husband in Wigan Parish Church under an elaborate medieval tomb.

The Mill Stone Inn is about 150 metres further along Standishgate which changes to Wigan Lane.

Return down Standishgate crossing at the lights to its southern end and enter the pedestrianised shopping area. Wallgate and its Station lie directly ahead.

15. The Croal Valley

An attractive linear walk along the wooded Croal valley to Moses Gate Country Park, Tonge Fold and Bolton, perfect for an afternoon stroll or winter morning.

Distance: 5 miles (8km)

Maps: Landranger 109; Pathfinder 712

Start: Kearsley Station

Finish: Bolton

Access: Regular Regional Railways trains from Bolton, Salford Crescent and Manchester Victoria. Monday to Saturdays only. Sundays catch bus service 8 from Manchester's Arndale Bus Station. Motorists should leave a car in Bolton and catch the train to Kearsley or park your car at Kearsley (A667) and catch the train back at the end of the walk.

The Pub

Ye Olde Man and Scythe. Perhaps the oldest continuously used tavern in Greater Manchester, the Man and Scythe occupies a site used as an inn since 1251. The present building dates from 1651 and has a colourful history, being captured by James Stanley, Earl of Derby, during the Civil War, who eventually defeated, spent his last night here before being beheaded by the Market Cross in Churchgate in 1651. A lively pub, very much part of the Bolton scene, offering Boddington's, Flower's and a variety of other real ales. Food available.

The Walk

Begin the walk outside Kearsley Railway Station. Go down the steps to the road and turn left down the hill under the magnificent railway bridge. Just before a row of terraced houses on the left, take the track on the left and go through the wooden stile straight ahead on to an attractive path which climbs up the railway embankment to follow the railway line.

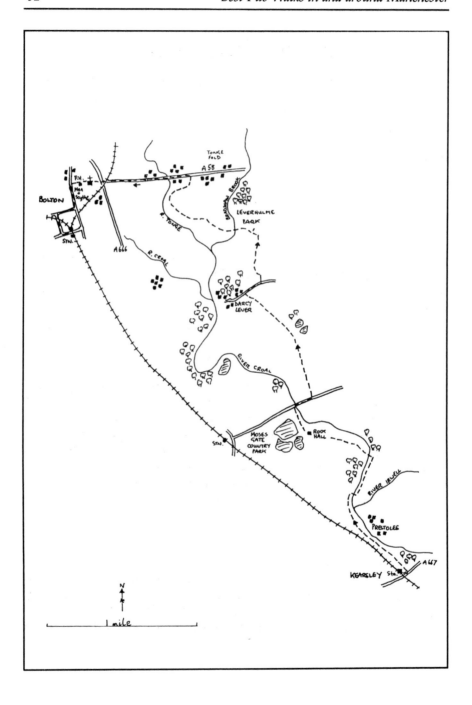

Down through the trees there are some lovely views to the River Croal below and a huge cotton mill at Presolee on the opposite river bank. Further along is a huge weir, a reminder of the days when many of Manchester's cotton mills were powered by water. The path passes the entrance to a short tunnel, continue up some steps and then turn right through Kearsley Country Park, following a path through woodland. Where the path joins a tarmac lane, turn right to a footbridge crossing the river.

Go over the bridge and turn left along the river bank across an area of scrub-land, Nob End. Nob End is a Nature Reserve by virtue of its lime rich soil, a legacy from when Wilson's Willow Works manufactured soda crystals in the 18th century and dumped their lime rich waste here. In the summer you'll find marsh orchid, broomrape and purging flax. The path continues along the river to a kissing gate. Continue straight ahead by the river until you reach a set of steps to the left signed 'Rock Hall'.

Go down the steps and follow a sandy path to a small footbridge across the river leading to parkland. Turn right and head for a small brick building ahead which are public toilets. At the toilets, turn left along the tarmac road past Rock Hall on the left. Rock Hall, once a Victorian mill owner's house, is now an excellent local information and countryside centre.

Where the path bends right, climb up the grassy embankment ahead to admire three lakes, the Crompton Lodges, conveniently surrounded by benches and picnic tables, and now a favourite fishing ground and home to a wide variety of geese, ducks and other bird-life.

Rejoin the road and continue along the road. Turn right over Farnworth Bridge and walk a short way up the road before turning left at a gateway signed Moses Gate Country Park. Since the 1960s, the local authority has undergone a massive land reclamation scheme to establish a country park planting over two million trees. It's now hard to imagine that most of this area was once derelict and the river heavily polluted. Follow the path until reaching a junction of paths. Take the second on the right up the hillside to a stile. Go over the stile and ignoring the path on the right, continue straight ahead following the main path along the river. The path leads to a road, turn right and go up the hill past the Levers Arms and then left along Bembridge Drive. Continue for a short distance and then turn right over the old railway bridge into the park.

Continue straight ahead to the sports grounds and race track and then turn left down the hill to a bridge. Cross the bridge and take the sandy path on the left, forking left to the cemetery. Where the path joins a tarmac path through the cemetery, turn left and follow the path alongside the river until it bends round to the Victorian Lodge at the Cemetery gates. Go through the gates and along Cemetery Road to emerge at a main road.

Cross the road with care and turn left to cross Tong Bridge, built in 1895. Walk along the road for about half a mile until a railway bridge crosses the road. Cross the road before the bridge taking the subway on the left under the busy A666. Follow the path round the parish church and turn left up the hill to Churchgate. On the left just beyond the parish church is Ye Olde Man and Scythe, a perfect place to end the walk.

To reach to the railway station, continue to the cross roads, turn left down Bradshawgate and then right up Moor Street to the bus and railway stations.

16. Tandle Hill

Tandle Hill lying between Rochdale,Middleton and Oldham, is an out-lier of the Pennines, and it provides a magnificent viewpoint and focal point of a popular Country Park.

Distance: 5 miles (8km)

Maps: Landranger 109, Pathfinder 713

Start: Mills Hill Station on the Manchester-Victoria Rochdale line (NB – NOT to be confused with Mill Hill on the Blackburn line)

Finish: Royton Town Centre

Access: Hourly Regional Railway services to Mills Hill on the Rochdale line (Sundays include); return on choices of frequent buses via Oldham to Manchester, also to Rochdale and Bolton Motorists should park on any station on Metrolink to access Victoria and the city centre (cheaper than parking in central Manchester).

The Pub

Tandle Hill Tavern (CAMRA listed) is rather special, a country pub only reached along a dirt track, a pub with very much a rural feel, in a building which was probably adapted from a Farmhouse. Beer is locally brewed Lees Mild, Bitter and (strong) Moonraker in the winter months. Food available include pie and peas. The Tavern is closed at most weekday lunchtimes in the winter months. As an alternative there is always the **Dog and Partridge** in Royton – see end of walk.

The Walk

Leave Mills Hill Railway Station via the steps down to the road. Cross the road and take the tarmac path opposite, to the left of the railway bridge. Go down the steps to cross an area of wasteland alongside a railway embankment. Where the path joins a muddy track, turn right. The path swings right past a farm house complete with its own duck

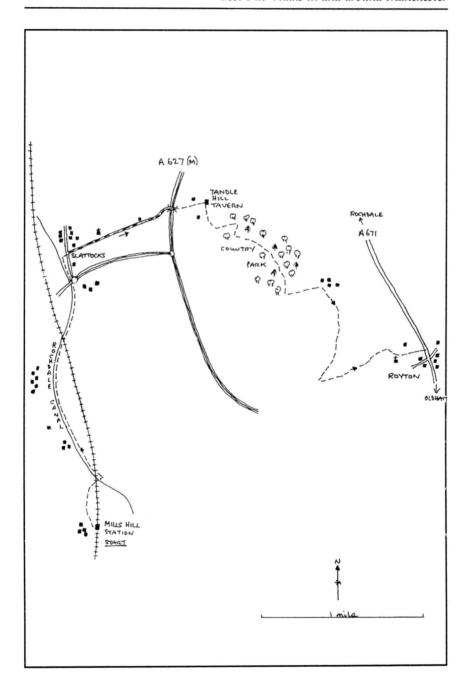

pond, and goes under the railway line to emerge at a canal bridge. Go over the bridge and then go down the steps on the right to join the canal tow-path.

Turn right and follow the Rochdale Canal under a huge blue painted railway bridge and on past a lock, one of the 92 locks required to carry the Rochdale Canal over the Pennines. The canal continues through pleasant farm land. Just beyond where the A664 road bridge crosses the canal, is a small bridge and building signed Slattock 54 Top Lock. Leave the canal here and join the road, cross and then continue in the same direction before turning left up Thornham Lane.

Thornham Lane is an attractive unsurfaced road lined with hedgerows. On the left is the handsome St John's Church and a little further up the lane, the surprisingly remote St John's primary school. The lane continues over a huge motorway bridge, before reaching Thornham Fold, a delightful hamlet of farms and cottages. At the far end of the hamlet is Tandle Inn Tavern.

After leaving the Tavern, return in the same direction to turn left from the Tavern and walk straight ahead to a wooden stile and field. Walk round the edge of the field, but when an iron fence comes into view, veer slightly left to join it 'and follow the fence, skirting round a stone obelisk to go through a wooden gate and then an iron gate to join a sandy path. Turn right and follow the path up to the obelisk which marks the summit of Tandle Hill.

In more recent years a metal plaque has been laid showing the various places which can be seen from Tandle Hill on a clear day – the huge power station at Fiddlers' Ferry, the Peak District hills and Manchester City Centre.

Turn left and take the steps down the hill through rhododendron bushes to a clearing in the woodland. Turn left and then immediately right to follow a path through attractive beech trees to an area of open grass land. Just past the wooden information shelter, turn right and follow the path straight ahead past a small copse of conifer trees. Ignore the path leading off right back up the hill, but continue straight ahead on a less well worn path down to a metal fence and track. Turn left along the track and continue for a short while until you reach a farm. Turn right down a stony path which runs next to a stream to emerge at a group of houses. Turn right again and follow the lane round, passing a modern house,'Birma House'.

Ignore the way marked footpath straight ahead, but turn left down a track following Oldham Way link path way markings to join a stream. Just past a group of wooden hen hutches is a small concrete bridge crossing the stream. Go over the bridge and up a stony track, after a few metres turn left along a path which drops down to a house. Continue straight ahead along a path running to the left of the house and through a wooden gate. Follow a sandy path with Royton Church spire in the distance. At a cross roads of paths, continue straight ahead to the road and turn right. Walk up the hill and where the road ends, go through a white metal gap stile and up some steps to the church. Turn left to a pedestrian crossing and Royton precinct. Go through the Precinct to the main road.

If you are unlucky enough to visit the Tandle Tavern on a weekday lunchtime when it is closed, try the CAMRA-listed Dog and Partridge on Middleton Road (close to the town centre) for a pint of Lees.

For buses to Rochdale and Bolton, turn left at the main road to the bus stop. For buses to Manchester and Oldham, cross the road and turn right to the bus stop just past the Railway Hotel opposite a garage.

17. Healey Dell and Watergrove

A walk on the northern edge of Rochdale, taking in Healey Dell Nature Reserve and the lost village of Watergrove.

Distance: 9 miles (15km) (circular)

Maps: Landranger 109; Pathfinder 701

Start and Finish: The Healey Hotel, Shawclough, off A671 north of Rochdale. Grid reference SD 885150

Access: Shawclough Road is the B6377, northwest of Rochdale Town centre. Regular daily buses 446/7 from Rochdale along Shawclough Road stop outside he Healey (Tel. 0161-228 7811 for timetable info.) Motorists should take the A671 signposted for Bacup and follow it to the mini-roundabout opposite Healey Mill (approx. 1$^1/_2$ miles). Turn left here along Shawclough Way, left again at the end along Shawclough Road. The Healey Hotel is on your left in 300 yards, there's ample roadside parking.

The Pub

The **Healey Hotel** is a small, virtually unspoilt end-of-terrace pub. Built sometime after the First War, it retains its original wall tiles, ornate wood panelled bar, tiled fireplaces and period style wall benches and fittings. Two small snugs add to the character of the place, the main bar area dominated by acres of wood panelling enclosing the staircase. Photographs of inter-war film stars dot the walls, with musical memorabilia bringing one wall into the 1960s. It's a Robinson's house, offering hand-pulled mild and best bitter, complemented in winter by a barrel of Old Tom stillaged beside the bar top. Meals are available at lunchtime, opening hours vary, but generally 12 noon – 3pm, 5pm (7 on Saturdays) – 11pm. A small beer garden is along the side and rear of the pub.

The Walk

Walk uphill from the Healey for about 200 metres to find Campion Way on the left. Follow this to the end, then continue along the footpath which soon merges with the old railway line on which new housing has been built. Simply remain with the old line as it strikes through small cuttings and over countless brooks. It's now heavily wooded, and there are glimpses through the trees revealing lodges at the old mill at Lower Fold (left) and the facade of Healey Hall (right), now a retirement home. The deep, wooded valley on your left is that of the River Spodden.

The old Rochdale to Bacup railway lasted around a century, opening in 1867 and closing in the mid-1960s. After years of neglect the trackbed was developed as a walkway and bridleway in the 1980s, offering spectacular views of the Spodden's deep gorge and of the surrounding moorland. The high point of the line is the graceful viaduct across the gorge, well over one hundred feet above the swirling torrents far below, and reached about half a mile into the walk.

Keep to the line beyond the viaduct, the interest of the deep, wooded gorge being replaced by wildflower-rich woodland and reedy old mill lodges. Look out for orchids, reedmace, iris and a profusion of dragon-flies and iridescent damselflies. Continue on through the old Broadley Station, remaining on the trackbed to and beyond its end (for about a mile), pass the bungalows and turn right up a side street here in Whitworth. At the main road, turn left to the Dog and Partridge and here turn right up Church Street with the one-way sign. Continue up Taylor Street through to Whitworth Square, the heart of the original weavers' hamlet, a splendid old fold of cottages adjoining one of the town's oldest pubs, The Red Lion (Tetley Bitter and Dark Mild, bar meals).

Climb the steps beyond The Red Lion, bear right with the path outside the graveyard wall and turn left up the surfaced road. The great tower of St Bartholomew's Church, until now largely hidden from view, commands the hillside to your left. Continue uphill as the road deteriorates, ignoring the turn to the golf club. Bear left along the first major moorland road (just before a small mound) and walk along the embankment alongside this.

The moorland you are now on is of modest height (never higher than 1000 feet) laced with an intricate web of paths and tracks, developed

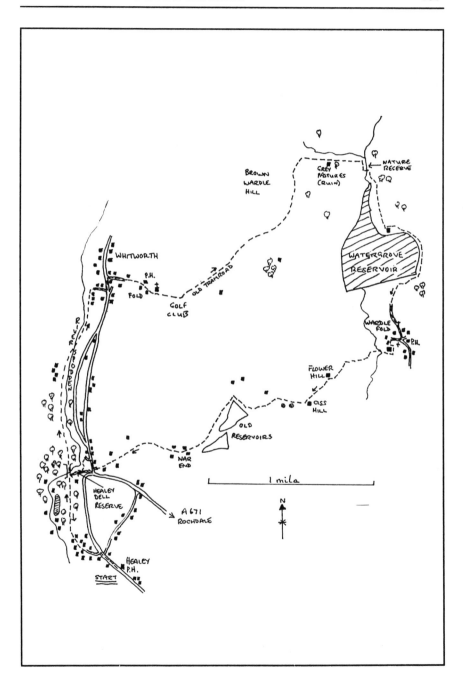

from the 1600s onwards to link innumerable small coal-mining and quarrying concerns, the melancholy remains of which dot the landscape. The lonely, winding moorland roads are enlivened in summer by numerous skylark, peewit, kestrel and curlew.

Stay with this track or bank, always heading for the break of slope on the right of Brown Wardle Hill, ahead. The embankment marks the line of a long-dead tram-road used to ferry coal and stone to local works in Whitworth. In about a mile, pass by shaley workings on your left. Allow the initial stretch of broken wall to fade away to the right and stay with the narrowing track-way. Pick up a further stretch of walling and follow this away from the track to the point where another wall plunges downhill at right-angles. Follow this down to the ruins of Grey Pasture Farm by the isolated tree.

Fallen farmsteads pepper the hillsides and moorland, their location often advertised by a stand of sycamores. They are largely the result of enforced clearance – "ecological cleansing" carried out when Watergrove Reservoir was constructed 60 years ago – to reduce threats of polluting the water catchment. The quarries, too, were closed down once stone for the reservoir dam had been obtained.

Continue downhill alongside the deepening defile of Longshoot Clough (on your left) to meet Higher Slack Brook. Go through the Nature Reserve gate just below the pond here and turn right. Cross the lower footbridge, follow the path up the side of the clough and through the wildflower meadow to reach the windsurfers' clubhouse and Warden's Office. The old cobbled lane disappearing under the waters was once the main street of the hamlet of Watergrove, drowned by the reservoir.

Watergrove Reservoir is Rochdale's main water supply and a popular windsurfing venue; incorporated into the surrounding wall are date-stones and lintels from farms and mills drowned or abandoned when the reservoir was constructed, some are over 300 years old.

Follow the access road around the reservoir, through the gates and down to Wardle Fold. This is another fine old weaving hamlet, now much expanded with in-filling and suburban development, but retaining many characteristic cottages and terraces. Look out for the village pub, a nameless building opposite the chapel hall. Turn right along Knowl Syke Street, to the right of the chapel hall, then left in front of Wardle House.

Shadows at Healey Dell

A homemade footpath sign directs you left to skirt round the side and rear of the old mill, the overgrown path eventually following a narrow brook and issuing onto a farm road. Turn left and follow this to its end at Flower Hill Farm. Follow the homemade signs through the somewhat chaotic farmyard and up the pastures beyond to the house on the skyline at Ciss Hill. Turn right along the walled track here and wind with it past a series of small ponds to a metalled road, thence ahead to a cattle grid. Bear half right across the rough land to a rough road along the foot of an old dam. Then bear right to the junction, then left along the rough road climbing slowly above the abandoned reservoirs of Brownhouse Wham and Homer Pasture.

Go slightly right (virtually straight over) at the rough crossroads at Nar End and along the roadway past chalet-bungalows to your right, continuing along the shallow valley. In half a mile, pass beneath the archway and descend to the main road at Healey Corner. Turn right up along the busy main road here and follow it for about 200 yards, looking on the left for Station Road. Turn down this and follow it to the bridge across the river Spodden. Immediately before this, go down the steps on your left to gain a path which descends gradually into the river gorge. At one point a side path descends, right, to a viewing point over a particularly scenic section of waterfalls, pot-holes and woodland, known locally as Fairies Chapel.

This whole area is Healey Dell Nature Reserve, a spectacular area of falls and shoots, great beech and oak woodland, ferns and damp-loving plants completely disguising what was once a locally important industrial site. Watermills existed here from Anglo-Saxon times, cotton and woollen mills survived until last century. Now delicate stone arches span the torrent and waterfalls eat into the gorge. Interpretive boards give an outline of the mill complexes which were once here; a bit of scrambling takes you to the weir beneath the viaduct, the start of a leat which once fed mills lower down the gorge, piles of tumbled masonry and the tunnel-like remains of old soughs. Keep an eye on the river for the sudden blue flash of a kingfisher or a white-bibbed dipper.

You should leave the gorge via a steep path from the narrow road immediately beneath the viaduct. Work up to this and follow the direction indicated by the wooden signpost up to the old railway line. Turn left along this (in other words, don't cross the viaduct) and retrace the first mile or so of the walk to return to the Healey.

18. Mills, Murders and Moorland

A taste of Greater Manchester's wilder Pennine countryside in and above Saddleworth and the Tame Valley, but also with a macabre touch that recalls a grim, unsolved 19th century murder.

Distance: 7¹/₂ miles (12km) − circular

Maps: Landrangers 109, 110. Pathfinders 702, 713

Start: Brownhills Visitor Centre, Uppermill. Grid reference SD 995066.

Access: Buses from Manchester, Oldham, Ashton-under-Lyne and Huddersfield pass the Visitor Centre. Tel. 0161 228 7811 for timetable information. Uppermill is about 4 miles ENE of Oldham along the A669/670. Parking is 300 metres north of Brownhills Visitor Centre on the A670, well signposted.

The Pubs

This walk passes such a plethora of excellent pubs that it would be churlish, to say the least, to feature one at the expense of others. In brief, the first one *en route* is the **Church Inn**, next to St Chad's, a capacious establishment offering Theakston's and Ind Coope beers (opening hours vary). A field path opposite this leads up to the Cross Keys Inn, claimed to be the oldest in Saddleworth (dating from about 1745) and offering Lees beers (open all day in summer, 11am − 3pm and 6.30pm − 11pm in winter). At Diglea **The Diggle Hotel** is an imposing old grit-stone building offering a range of beers from Timothy Taylor's and Bodding-ton's (open 11am − 3pm and 7pm − 11pm, all day Saturdays). The **Horse and Jockey** at Bleak Hey Nook is a remarkable old moorland pub, don't let the rather drab exterior prevent you experiencing its depths if you find it open (Mon-Sat evenings about 7pm − 11pm and Sat lunchtimes); with two cosy rooms liberally dotted with settees, armchairs, old tables and benches, warmed by colossal open fires in the winter and offering an ever-changing choice of real ales. Others include the Swan in Dob-cross Square and the Navigation, just up the road from Brownhills car park.

The Walk

The walk commences at the Brownhills Visitor Centre car park (bus travellers alight near the Visitor Centre itself). Beside the entrance to the car park is the Wool Road Transhipment Shed. This modest structure was the place where bales of wool, worsted, cotton and other goods from the Manchester area were unloaded from narrow-boats and transferred to strings of pack horses which then carried the goods over the Pennines to the north-eastern section of the canal at Marsden, about six miles away. This practice occurred between the opening of the canal in 1799 and the completion of the Standedge Canal Tunnel. The car park marks the site of a larger warehouse while an old mill opposite is now converted into luxury housing.

The Huddersfield Narrow Canal was opened throughout in 1811 and abandoned (in common with many others) by Act of Parliament in 1944, but had been essentially disused for several decades before this. It is called "Narrow" to distinguish it from the Huddersfield Broad Canal, still in use in the Huddersfield area. The difference is the width of the locks, on the Narrow canal they are 7' and can take one narrow-boat, while on the Broad canal they are 14' and can take two, side by side. A very active Canal Society is gradually restoring the canal in piecemeal fashion, the short stretch followed by this walk is fully reopened and a trip boat runs at weekends between the car park, Visitor Centre and Uppermill village.

Walk south along the tow-path, the canal on your right, to reach the Brownhills Visitor Centre immediately beyond the overbridge. The Centre lies huddled beneath and between canal, railway, river and road, each reflecting the long established importance of this route across the South Pennines. Open daily except Mondays, the Centre has a wealth of information and exhibitions concerning the natural history and industrial heritage of this Upper Tame Valley; it's a base, too, for the Countryside Wardens and for frequent guided walks.

From the front of the Centre, turn left and walk along the main road (back towards the car park) to reach the turning "circle" on your right. Take the rough lane which rises from this circle just to the right of the garden gate to house no. 20 (NOT the canal tow-path). At the hairpin bend, continue ahead along the grassy path, soon reaching and crossing the railway line (take care, it's an unguarded crossing!). Then follow the

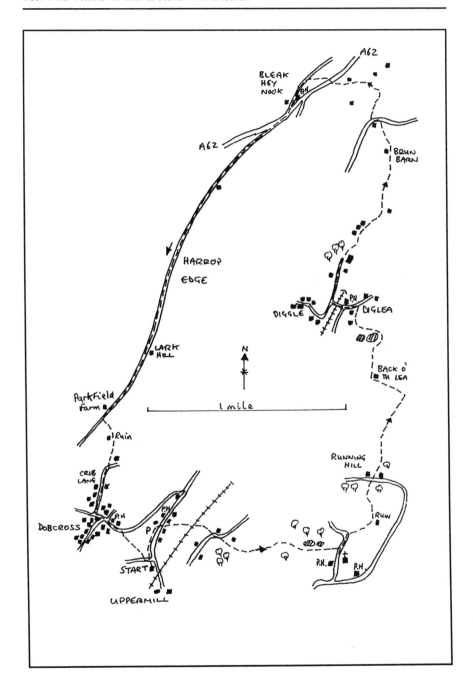

waymarked path through the gates up the hillside to reach a narrow road beside a barn and cottages.

Walk ahead for a few yards, past some cottages on your left. At the bend go straight ahead along the driveway towards Ryefields. Within yards a footpath sign points right, through the fence, and down to a lower road. On reaching this turn left, then go along the track to the right of the driveway. Pass through the gap stile and walk ahead, keeping the wall close to your left. Follow this field-side path, climbing gently towards Saddleworth's parish church, the wall or fence occasionally changing from left to right. Cross the beck and follow the obvious path up the hillside, bearing right at the split above the pond, one of two old mill lodges associated with two long-gone small scribbling mills (places where raw wool was combed, or scribbled, to make it easier to work before despatch to larger weaving mills). On reaching the road below the church tower, turn right to the church car parking area and the Church Inn, one of the hamlet's two pubs; the other, the Cross Keys, can be glimpsed at the top end of the pasture above the Church Inn.

St Chad's church stands in splendid isolation on the hillside high above the village and marks the site of the original hamlet in the area, built when the valley below was still well wooded. The current building of weather-beaten, darkened grit-stone is a Victorian replacement for an original one founded in 1200. Beside the churchyard wall are the old village stocks, about 300 years old, while the building between the church and the pub is the old hearse house dated 1824.

On the second weekend following August 12th (usually August Bank Holiday Saturday and Sunday) each year, locals celebrate with gusto the Longwood Thrump Rushcart Festival. This revived medieval fair recalls the days when most churches and chapels had floors made of nothing more than compressed earth or clay. As a celebration of the annual cycle of the renewal of the seasons, local people gathered rushes to be strewn over the floor of the church, giving thanks for this renewal – and also refreshing the atmosphere of the church and providing a warm, dry flooring. Before being spread, the rushes were paraded through all the villages in Saddleworth on a beautifully rush-bedecked and decorated haywain hauled by teams of locals, morris and rapper dancers followed by a service at St Chad's. The saying "Going on the waggon" – steering clear of alcohol – is said to originate here, the balance and skill needed to climb onto and stay on the Rushcart proscribing any consumption of beer, cider or spirits!

Weavers' cottages tumble steeply down from Dobcross Square

The churchyard and cemetery opposite are gloriously overgrown, tombstones and monuments rising eerily, often drunkenly from the surrounding greenery. One gravestone (in the south-west corner of the graveyard behind the hearse house) recalls the "Bill o' Jacks" murders, an incident when the landlord (William, son of Jack – hence the name) and his son were murdered at a now demolished isolated moorland pub, the Moorcock Inn. The gravestone records "Here lie the dreadfully bruised and lacerated bodies of William Bradbury and Thomas his son who were together savagely murdered in an unusually horrid manner on Monday night, April 2, 1832..." The culprit was never apprehended – the funeral of the victims drew an audience estimated at 10,000, swelled to such levels by intense interest generated by the regional press; upwards of 30,000 are said to have visited the scene of the macabre killings within days of the event.

Retrace your steps along the road to the left of the church tower and walk downhill to the sharp left-hand bend. Take the second drive on the right (there's a broken old footpath sign here) and walk up behind the white cottage to the concreted part of the drive to your right. This leads up to a narrow, walled footpath. Climb the two low stiles at the top and walk up the sunken track, boggy to begin with. On your left and about 50 yards below the ruined Wickens Farm is a waymark arrow, yellow on blue with a blue owl emblem (the sign of the Oldham Way Footpath). Bear left here, pass below the ruins and cross the small stone-slab bridge in the clough (waymarked). Ford the boggy area in the alders at the far end of the pasture and walk ahead, following the right-hand crest of the defile. Look half right near the end to locate the high ladder stile and climb this.

Turn right up the narrow road, then go almost immediately left along the narrow, signposted footpath which winds between the garage and a laurel hedge. Skirt the bottom end of the garden beyond, climb the stile and continue along the wide path at the foot of the field. Go through the gap stile and head for the telegraph pole, then pass through the small kissing gate beside the red field gate at this corner. Walk along with the wall on your right, go through the gate at the corner and turn left. Keep the wall on your left, ignore the first gate and continue to the far corner. Turn left here along the walled greenway and walk to the isolated cottages at Back o'th Lee.

Once through the white gate beyond these cottages, turn right and walk down the line of the wall on your right to the corner, pass through the gap and walk to the bottom end of the field. Climb the stile near the telegraph pole and skirt the right hand edge of this rough enclosure (a drained mill lodge), leaving by the unusual wooden gate at the bottom. Turn left, ford Diggle Brook and pass through the bridleway gate at the far side of the paddock. Bear slightly right to find a further, yellow metal gate, remaining with the path beyond this to emerge beside a house.

This is Diglea hamlet, a glorious survival of weavers' cottages and yeomans' houses. The hamlet once boasted several mills, part of one still exists beside the isolated chimney visible towards the head of the valley. Abandoned leats, lodges and silted water features passed on the walk recall other old mills. Turn left down the road and follow it past the Diggle Hotel and over the wide railway bridge.

Boat Lane, the old road beside the Diggle Hotel, recalls the days when barge horses were led up here and over Standedge Edge along the Boat Lane, while the narrow-boats were propelled through the tunnel beneath by professional "Leggers." This tunnel runs beneath the rail tunnels visible from the railway bridge beyond the hotel. Completed in 1811, Standedge Canal Tunnel is, at over 3 miles, the longest (and highest) in Britain. Currently disused, there are long term plans to reopen this inspired engineering feat and reinstate the Huddersfield Narrow as one of three trans-Pennine waterways. Its portal is about 100 metres south of the railway bridge.

Turn right along Harrop Court Road and follow this through the Fold and past the mill, bearing right along the no through road to reach the entrance to Harrop Court Farm. At this point go straight ahead up the short grassy track, the barn on your right. Go through the gap stile beside the gate on your left, then walk to and cross the footbridge beneath the trees. Look ahead to the narrow, fenced off valley. There's a wire-mesh gate through this fence, once through, bear half right and follow the path up past the lone thorn tree, through the broken wall and then uphill alongside this to the farmhouse at Brun Barn.

From here are extensive views across Saddleworth and down the deep trough the Tame has cut into the grit-stone plateau. Ahead, right the spoil tip topped by the large circular brick structure marks the course of the railway tunnel far below, the bricks are the top of a ventilation shaft.

Just beyond the farmhouse is a homemade footpath sign on the left, climb the stile here and walk ahead to the drive, following this up to the road. Turn left and go downhill for about 100 metres. At the left hand bend turn right and go down the rough road, winding through this valley and past several houses to reach the main A62. Cross straight over this and go along the green lane opposite, keeping left to pass behind the white-painted Horse and Jockey Inn.

Walk ahead to and along the main A62 towards Oldham, bearing left in 200 metres or so along the rough, narrow Harrop Edge Lane. The gentle climb up Harrop Edge opens out extensive views across to the heights of Saddleworth Moor, the spectacular gash of the Chew Valley and the area's war memorial, an obelisk on a hill top known as Pots and Pans. Off to your right are the two reservoirs at Castleshaw, the humps and ditches of a Roman fortlet may easily be spotted this side of the upper one, particularly if a low sun high-lights the shadows.

Crest the summit level of this by-road and continue on past Lark Hill, the road becoming surfaced. Pass by the cream painted Parkfield farm on your right, some 75 yards or so after this, fork left along the rough road and wind with this past the fallen barn. Soon after the track begins to descend, turn right along the narrow road, Crib Lane, guarded by width restriction signposts, following this down into Dobcross, bearing left to reach the Swan Inn.

The heart of Dobcross village, the oldest in the area, is the glorious village square at the top of the steep main street, hemmed in by three storey weavers' houses – there must be more mullions here than anywhere else in England. On the door lintel of the Swan Inn, overlooking the square, are carved the initials BW & SW, 1765. These were members of the Wrigley family; a descendant emigrated to the USA where he developed and established the chewing gum company that still bears the family name. The village, a maze of back lanes and ginnels, featured heavily in the Hollywood film "Yanks" and is well worth taking time to explore thoroughly.

With the Swan Inn to your left, follow Sugar Lane out of the village. At the corner 150 metres away, bear right down Nicker Brow, walking down this back road to the railings. Follow the steep footpath beyond these and walk down to the old water mill beside the main road, turning left along this to reach the junction beside Brownhills Visitor Centre. Should you wish to visit Uppermill, turn right along the road to reach the village centre, returning to the car park via the canal tow-path.

19. The Medlock Valley

A walk along the Medlock valley, using part of the Medlock Valley Way, from the outskirts of Oldham and edge of the Pennine hills to the very heart of Manchester city centre.

Distance: 9 miles (15km)

Maps: Landranger 109; Pathfinder 713, 724.

Start: Oldham Mumps Railway Station

Finish: Manchester Piccadilly

Access: Regular trains from Manchester Victoria to Oldham Mumps (weekdays only) Sundays bus 82 from Oldham Street (near Piccadilly) Motorists should park at any Metrolink Station and travel to/from Victoria/Piccadilly by Metrolink.

The Pub

The Jolly Angler, Ducie Street. This classic Manchester back street local is something of *cause celèbre* among Manchester pub afficionados. Threatened by a proposed redevelopment linked to the Manchester 1993 Olympic bid, local community groups and environmentalists joined forces to keep the developers at bay. The one room interior is barely larger than a modest sized house parlour, a corner bar serving two distinct areas, one half given over to pool and darts, the other with simple wall benches and tables, warmed by a roaring fire. Folk groups, often with an Irish bent, regularly ensure that the pub is crowded, the main draw otherwise being the well kept selection of Hyde's beers – hand pulled mild, light and bitter with a barrel of Anvil Old Ale often gracing the bar in the winter.

The Walk

Begin the walk outside Oldham Mumps Railway Station. Turn right towards a large pedestrian bridge over the busy dual carriageway. Go up the first incline, but rather than cross the road, continue across a

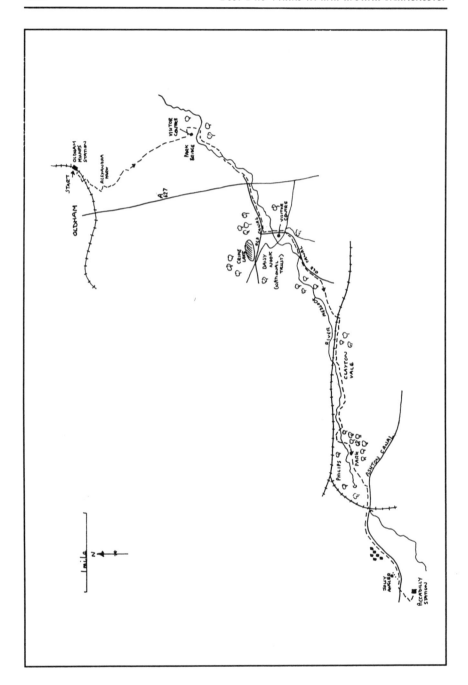

metal bridge, painted blue, over the railway and then turn immediately right. Walk past an all weather playing field and then continue straight ahead between houses, Marlborough Street, to the main road. Cross the road and turn right and then turn down Woodstock Road to another main road. Cross the road to the park and go through the main gates on the left into the park.

Turn right to the pond and then left passing an attractive rose garden and recently-built adventure playground. In the distance, on the right hand side, is a elegant Victorian pagoda, erected in 1899 to celebrate the fifty years of the incorporation of Oldham Borough.

Just past the playground, take the second path on the right down some steps through an attractive wooded vale to a gate. Go through the gate, cross the road and walk across the grass to a dismantled railway track. Turn left to walk under a road tunnel and continue straight ahead to join a tarmac road. From here there are some magnificent views of the surrounding hills, including Hartshead Pike, marking the eastern edge of the Medlock Valley.

Now keep to main track where it swings left and take a path on the right to a gap stile in a fence. Turn left to follow a muddy path round the edge of a field and through woodland before descending to a row of terrace houses (Dingle Terrace). Go down the hill past the Stables Visitor Centre on the right to Park bridge, where once there was an iron works. You can still see the huge chimney and remains of the iron foundry which was established in the 1780s and continued in production until 1963. The Stables Visitor Centre was once the iron master's stables and has an exhibition about the Iron Works.

Cross over the bridge and follow the road just past the factory and then take the path on the right which runs parallel with the road, before rejoining it just before a bridge. Cross the bridge and go through the stile on the left and follow a path along the river past the imposing 19th century Thomas Kerfoot's Chemical Works and under a road bridge to join a canal tow-path.

This is the Fairbottom Branch Canal, one of a number of canals linking into the Ashton Canal. Much of the canal is now over grown with bulrushes and other wetland loving plants. Just before reaching a wonderful circular lock system, go down the steps on the right to cross an aqueduct over the river. Continue straight ahead into Daisy Nook Country Park, a area of attractive woodland which has become the most popular part of the valley. The village was originally called Waterhouses, but after Ben Brierley wrote 'A day out at Daisy Nook' the name was adopted, with Daisy Nook becoming a popular excursion for local mill workers. The path continues to the John Howarth Visitor Centre opened in 1987 which has exhibitions on the Valley's wildlife, flora and canal system.

Continue past the Visitor Centre through the car park to the main road. Cross the main road and walk straight ahead to join the tow-path along the Hollingwood Branch Canal, also built to link with the Ashton Canal. As with the Fairbottom Branch Canal, a number of collieries were established along the canal and it became an flourishing transport link for the local textile and iron industries. Today, it is an important habitat for a rich variety of plants and fresh water life including dragonflies. On the right is the River Medlock meandering through the river plain.

At Cinderland Bridge turn right through a stile and follow a farm track path heading towards some electricity pylons. Walk between them and look for a wooden stile on the right. Follow a narrow path along the edge of a steep slope alongside the river. Across the river is Brookdale Golf Course. Cross a small wooden bridge and go over the stile to meet a path dropping down to the River Medlock. Turn left up the hill over a footbridge crossing a railway line and then turn right along an attractive wooded path along the side of some houses which emerges at a street. Turn right and then right again to follow a wooded path down the hill, emerging at a cobbled lane leading down to a road. On the right hand side is the Bay Horse pub (which serves food).

Cross the road and follow a sandy track past a small hut, used by the Medlock Valley wardens, and through Clayton Vale. This area was once used for tipping ash from a nearby power station together with shale and domestic rubbish. The tipping stopped in 1971 and the area is gradually being transformed. Just before an overgrown pond, cross a brick bridge and follow the path along a cutting to a disused railway bridge and embankment which once carried a branch line from the main Sheffield, Ashton, Manchester Railway to Stuart Street Power Station and Clayton Aniline Chemical Works.

Go up the steps on the right which lead to the top of the bridge and continue along the bridge to the far side where a second set of steps leads down to a road. Cross the road and opposite is the entrance to Philip's Park. Philip's Park was one of the first formal parks to be laid out in the country. It was named in honour of Mark Philip, M.P for Manchester City and officially opened on 22nd August 1846.

Go through the park and just before the main exit, turn left up to an ornate fountain. At the road, turn left again and go over the bridge by the old lock keeper's house (1865). This is the entrance to the canal tow path. Re-cross the canal and turn left to follow the canal tow-path of the Ashton canal, built in 1799 to link the Rochdale Canal in Manchester with the Peak Forest and Huddersfield Canals in Ashton.

From here it is a pleasant, level walk into the centre of Manchester, emerging at Paradise Wharf, with its canal-side development and recently built luxury waterside apartments. You merge on Ducie Street. About 100 metres on the right, on the opposite side of the road, is the Jolly Angler, while it's less than five minutes walk to the left to Piccadilly Station for trains or trams.

20. Stalybridge and Walkerwood Reservoir

A circular canal and moorland walk with a real Pennine flavour, following the Huddersfield Narrow Canal and finishing on the edge of Hollingworthall Moor by Walkerwood Reservoir with panoramic views across the western Pennine uplands and Greater Manchester.

Distance: 8 miles (12km)

Maps: Landranger 109, Pathfinder 724

Start and finish: Stalybridge Railway Station

Access: Frequent Manchester Piccadilly (Trans-Pennine Express) and local services from Victoria on the Greenfield/Huddersfield/Wakefield line serve Stalybridge. Motorists can reach the station easily, just off the A635, with plenty of parking nearby.

The Pub

Perhaps the most celebrated railway station buffet in England, **Stalybridge Station Buffet** (CAMRA listed) is a railway and real ale buffs' delight – an unspoiled Victorian railway buffet uses, Batemans and guest beers from elsewhere, plus bottled Belgian beers. Railway memorabilia, a book and magazine shelf to browse or buy, a real fire, and a very friendly atmosphere – Ken, the manager, continues a family tradition of hospitality. Hot snacks are usually available – a house speciality is pie and black peas – a delicacy unique to Lancashire/north Cheshire. This living piece of railway heritage is constantly threatened by faceless bureaucrats determined to close the business by sky-rocketing the rent, as well as reducing a once busy local link, now Britain's (and perhaps Europe's) worst rail service, the weekly, one directional Stockport-Stalybridge Friday only service (the Timetable now a mere footnote in BR Table 90). Reductions in service explain why the Buffet no longer opens on Sunday lunchtimes. If you do arrive at the wrong time, the **White House** (CAMRA listed) in Water Street, with Banks and Theakston's may be some compensation.

The Buffet, Staylbridge Station

The Walk

Leave Stalybridge Station and head under the rail bridge and along the main road into the town. Just before the bridge crossing the river Tame, there is a fine stone portico with two plaques commemorating the Chartist leader, Joseph Raynor Stephens (1805-1879), and the Plug Plot Riots of 1842, when in a bid to persuade Parliament to reform the electoral system, radical Chartist campaigners removed the plugs from factory boilers all over Lancashire and in parts of Yorkshire, rendering them useless.

Just before the bridge, by a small garden is a path leading down to the river. Follow this path, crossing the car park to join a road. Cross the road and turn right over a bridge and walk towards the traffic lights ahead. On the left, just before the road junction, is a small landscaped area where the canal starts. Turn left up the tow-path.

This is part of the Huddersfield Narrow Canal, linking Huddersfield in West Yorkshire with Ashton in Tameside and opened in 1811. The canal

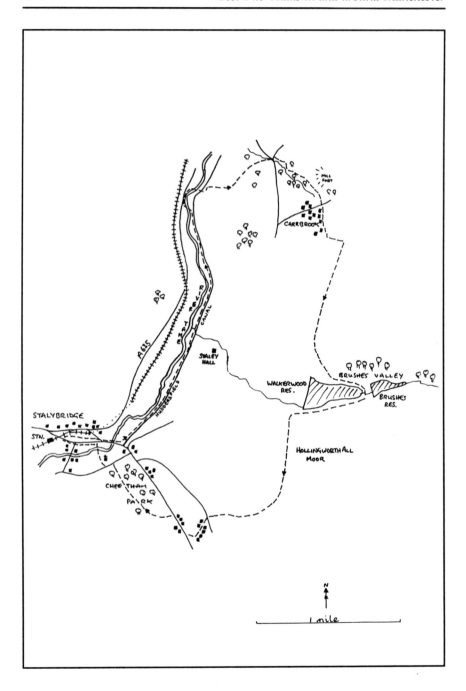

was the brain child of John Ramsden, a major Huddersfield landowner and entrepreneur who wanted to link the textile town of Huddersfield with Manchester and thereby create the shortest Trans-Pennine waterway. The canal proved to be a major engineering feat, taking seventeen years to complete, with a three mile (5km) tunnel under Standedge while canal barge-men, known as 'leggers' literally pushed the barge along the narrow tunnel, using their legs against its walls. The canal was finally closed in 1944 and many sections were filled in and locks allowed to deteriorate. In recent years the Huddersfield Narrow Canal Society has begun to restore the canal, repairing locks and digging up weed choked sections.

The first half mile of the canal is dominated by a huge electric substation, creating a landscape of huge pylons and overhead wires. The canal has been diverted for a short section, but the path continues straight ahead under huge pylons to rejoin the canal a little further ahead.

Where the tow-path joins the road, cross and continue along the canal. From this point, the canal becomes a delightful wooded corridor, climbing steadily towards the Pennines with a series of locks which have recently been refurbished. The canal then continues through a short tunnel. At this point you can either enjoy an exciting walk through the tunnel, a torch is advised despite the welcome handrail, or continue over the canal via a small concrete bridge, to follow a sandy path over the tunnel.

If you decided to go through the tunnel, continue through the tunnel to the lock ahead. Just before the lock is a small concrete bridge over the canal, cross this and double back alongside the canal, past some enormous wooden sculptures in the shape of leaves, to join some steps by the tunnel mouth. Go up the steps and turn left to rejoin the same path followed by those not wishing to explore the gloomy pleasures of the canal tunnel. Continue to a gate and stile. Go through the stile and walk straight ahead through the remains of an old railway bridge towards a farm.

Go past the farm and walk straight towards a golf course, but before reaching the wire fence, turn sharp left up a steep slope, crossing a small muddy stream with the help of some rather well hidden planks of wood, and continue to a wooden gap stile.

Take the path on the right and then where the path forks, take the right fork towards a row of houses. Walk past the houses to join a road, and continue up the hill to a main road. A few yards on the left is the Stamford Arms – also recommended – which serves food and a variety of beers.

Otherwise cross the road and follow a track straight ahead. From here there are superb panoramic of Buckton Moor to the left and to the right, views down the Tame Valley. The track joins a road, and continues through a gate and past some 18th century cottages with attractive mullioned windows. Continue straight ahead, passing a school on the right and some modern housing (ignoring a fork to the left) before reaching a main road.

Cross the main road and walk straight ahead up a stony track (ignoring the path signed 'Stalybridge Country Park'). Where the track swings sharp right at a farm house,'The Fold' go through a wooden gate on the left and follow a clear green path up the field to join another stony track. Turn right up the track and follow it for about half a mile with the track becoming a tarmac road.

Where the road bends sharply down hill, take a green track on the left to a metal gate. Go through the gate and follow this green lane down the hill to Walkerwood reservoir below, set in a wooded basin.

At the road, cross over and take the path almost opposite to the reservoir. Walk along the path around the bottom of the dam. Then follow the path around the edge of the reservoir thorough attractive woodland and the occasional rhododendron bush which then becomes open moorland and heather.

The path continues past the reservoir before joining the road at a stone stile. Do not cross this stile but continue for 70 metres to a second stile. Ignore this to turn sharp left up the hill to a fence and stile by an old brick building, a former rifle range. Cross the stile and follow the main path past the building, keeping in the same direction towards a group of pylons in the distance. Continue past a metal gate and stile on the left, following a sunken path to a wooden stile on the right. Go over the stile and pass a holly bush to a gate and stile. On the right are magnificent views across Ashton and Stalybridge.

Go over the stile and continue along the lane past stables and a farmhouse to a gate on the right. Go through the gate and descend the field to a narrow gap stile at the bottom corner of the field directly ahead. Continue in the same direction, past more holly bushes, to join a track which meets the road. Cross the road and turn right. After a few metres there is a track on the left between houses, which follows the road round to a street named Quarry Clough. Turn right down the hill, emerging at a main road. Cross with care.

Turn right. 200 metres beyond the Hare and House pub, turn left through a gateway into a park. Follow the main tarmac path down to a bridge overlooking Eastwood RSPB Nature Reserve. Cross the bridge and follow the path up the hill round the edge of the Nature Reserve to the main park. Turn right down the hill past the playground into Stalybridge. At the park entrance, continue along a minor road to the main road. Cross the road and turn left and then right down Trinity Street into the Market Square and past the Parish Church. Continue straight ahead over the bridge and take the first left, Market Street, back to Stalybridge Railway Station.

21. Arden Hall and Haughton Dale

A lovely riverside and woodland walk close to the urban heart of Stockport and Manchester – and with a unexpected link with William Shakespeare.

Distance: 6$\frac{1}{2}$ or 9 miles (10 or 15km)

Maps: Landranger 109; Pathfinder 724.

Start: Bredbury Station

Finish: Romiley Station

Access: Both Bredbury and Romiley Stations are on the Manchester Piccadilly-New Mills Central/Sheffield line; Romiley is also served by Rose Hill-Piccadilly trains. Frequent service. Bredbury Station is alongside the A560 Stockport-Hyde road about 2$\frac{1}{2}$ miles ENE of Stockport town centre – large free car park at Bredbury (frequent return trains or 1$\frac{1}{2}$ mile walk).

The Pub

The **Railway Inn** at Romiley is both welcome and welcoming at the end of this exploration of the Lower Tame Valley. It's open all day (standard Sunday hours) so you can count on an excellent pint or two of Stockport's best as a refresher before tackling the steep stairs up to the adjoining station. Robinson's' Best Bitter, Mild and Old Tom are all hand-pulled from a central bar in this traditional, multi-roomed local, largely unaltered since its erection in the Edwardian era – there's even that increasingly rare survival in today's suburban pub, an "outside" (gents) toilet. Rumour has it that a spectre stalks the building (maybe a glass or two too many of Old Tom . . .). The new licensees offer a genuine, friendly welcome to mud-spattered, thirsty walkers (and their dogs and children) as well as excellently kept beers (though no pub food when last visited, in April 1994), in this unpretentious, no-nonsense "basic" local.

A "rocky" ascent from Gibraltar to the Peak District canal!

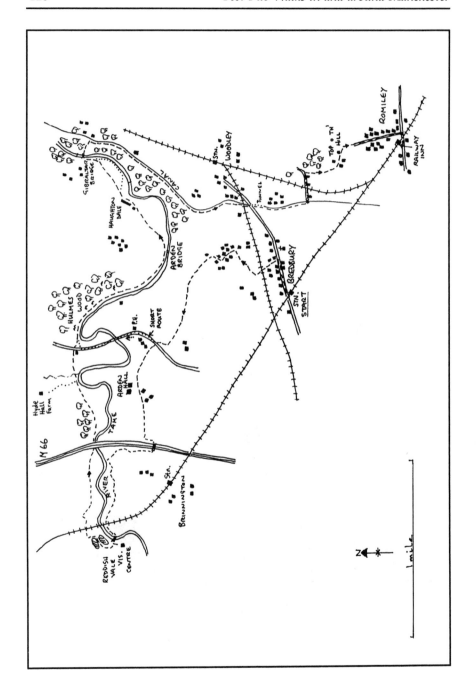

The Walk

Although the initial stages of this walk are largely through uninspiring housing and past industrial premises, once into the Tame Valley itself, the walk takes on a completely different character. The shorter walk option excludes a visit to the Valley Information Centre and associated wildfowl lakes.

Leave Bredbury station car park and turn right in front of the Rising Sun pub, following Stockport Road East for about a quarter of a mile. As you reach the graveyard, cross the main road and search out the narrow pathway between house numbers 48 and 50 (on your left). Follow this fenced path over the old railway line then bear right across the recreation ground, heading for the new, low red-roof-tiled sheltered housing at the far side. Walk along the short access road to the playing fields beside this building and turn left along Mill Lane. Remain with this road, pass Lowick Green road on your left, then bear right with Mill Lane, following it to its end at playing fields; go left along the cindered track, where the tarmac ends.

In about 150 metres, climb the stile beside the gate on your left and follow the muddy, hedged path to reach rough pasture. Trace the well worn path across this, regaining a wide hedged path at the far side (roughly in line with the right-hand edge of the warehouses). Stay with this old field road past further stiles until a point about 100 metres before the main road would be reached. Look on your right here for a solid wooden stile, climb this and bear half left towards the red-brick terrace in the middle distance, crossing straight over the main road to reach this terrace.

Follow the footpath sign for Reddish Vale and pass by the terrace to your right. A further 200 metres along this, Battle Lane, brings you to the driveway to Arden Hall (private). The strange looking, semi-derelict Arden Hall (also known as Harden Hall) was built for members of the Arden family (relatives of Shakespeare's mother) who moved up from Warwickshire. The existing structure dates from about 1597 and was protected by a deep moat, but was abandoned around Christmas 1822 when it started collapsing. Once famed for the collection of paintings kept there, its great hall was said to hold over 200 diners. It was christened Cromwell's Castle during the Civil War as the owner was a Parliamentary supporter in a predominantly Royalist neighbourhood.

Tradition has it that Oliver Cromwell himself was a house guest. Battle Lane is named after a skirmish which supposedly occurred here during the Civil War.

For the shorter walk, retrace your steps to the terrace and turn left down Castle Hill, regaining the main road virtually opposite the Arden Arms. Bear left along the road, cross the bridge and causeway and cross to the right, taking the path into the woodland on the right at the lay-by.

For the longer walk, remain with the rough, pot-holed Battle Lane until it bends left into the top end of the industrial estate (about 200 yards). At this point walk ahead (below the sewage works), to find almost immediately a further signpost for Reddish Vale. From here a new path has been created to replace one largely lost beneath the new section of motorway ahead. Walk to the motorway fence and turn left with the waymark arrow, following the surfaced path to and over the long footbridge across the motorway. At the far end, walk ahead a few paces and turn right, tracing the path along the top edge of the wooded clough which, eventually, falls down to the flood-plain of the river Tame. Turn left and wind with the path through the bottom end of the woods here.

These pleasant woods are a riot of colour in late spring, undergrowth thick with bluebells, yellow lesser celandine, the pungent white ramson (wild garlic) and pinky-red herb robert and red campion. Squeeze through the stile at the end of the wood, turn up the bank and then bear right with the signpost for the Visitor Centre. The path joins the river-bank beneath the graceful railway viaduct (built in 1874/5) and crosses the river bridge 150 yards further on to reach the Reddish Vale Visitor Centre on your left. It's normally open daily except Fridays and houses a mine of information about the Lower Tame Valley, its history and natural attractions.

Amongst these natural attractions are the varied wildfowl found on the old mill lodges near the Centre, great crested grebe and tufted duck amongst them. Follow the path past the sign-board for the Bottom Mill Pond and alongside the water to the Upper Pond, then walk along the embankment between the two. The lodges (ponds) are virtually all that remains of a considerable calico printing works which flourished here.

Climb the stile and turn left along the track, then right in about 75 yards at the gate cum stile, climbing this muddy bridleway beneath the viaduct. Wind with it around its double-bends, then look on the right for a stile signposted "Stockport Road." Take this and trail through the rough pasture, then descend the steps through thorn woodland to the marshy meadows in the valley bottom, well blessed with reeds such as Phragmites and Reedmace (Bullrush) during summer. Simply remain with the path beneath the motorway bridge, winding past reedy ponds and following the occasional signpost for Stockport Road. One signpost offers the chance of a short diversion up beside a wooded clough to give a distant view of the medieval Hyde Hall Farm, one of the oldest secular buildings in Greater Manchester (private, no access).

The main route continues downstream some way above the Tame, eventually issuing onto Stockport Road beside a red-brick house. Cross straight over, turn downhill then in a few yards go left at the footpath sign for Meadow Lane, crossing the butterbur-infested pasture to the riverside bridleway and turning upstream along it (this is where the shorter walk rejoins the main route).

The woods clothing the steep valleyside here are Hulme's Wood, disguising very well the scant remains of the once important coal-mining industry which thrived in this little known, far-flung corner of the Lancashire and North Cheshire coalfield. On the left here was Hulmes Colliery while across the river and a little upstream was Bredbury Colliery; the woodland also hosted many small bell-pits (as opposed to collieries proper), so-named because of the shape of the working, miners simply digging a vertical shaft (the bell "handle") and delving out the coal beneath. Mining in this area commenced in the 1550s and lasted until 1929. Within the majestic beechwoods you can still see the occasional small spoil-heap or old shaft capped by a block of concrete, while soughs (drains) still issue into the river

The walk now more or less follows the river through the shallow gorge it has cut into the shales and sandstone, natural woodland supplemented by new plantings of birch and spruce. The substantial footbridge a short way above the weir (which supplied the long-gone Arden Mill) is Arden Bridge; one of the large boulders in the river here is known as Robin Hood's Stone, said to have been flung here by the medieval rogue from Werneth Low, some two miles away, whilst in a rage! Beyond Arden Bridge (do not cross) the Tame meanders in great sweeps to the far side of the valley floor, leaving the path to climb slightly to old houses and cottages at Haughton Dale. The pleasant pastures and copses here were once an industrial complex known as the Meadow Factory. Built in 1790 it made its name as a wire-works, being the largest in the world in the 1880s. It closed in 1903 and was demolished some years later, leaving Haughton Dale House (dating from 1713) and the employees' terrace in peaceful solitude.

Cross the narrow road and walk along the front of these cottages at Ivy Terrace, continuing past the small enclosures beyond and bear left along the main path at the end. Keep on for about 200 yards to the end of the stand of willow and alder trees growing on and above the near river bank. On the right here a squeezer stile leads off the main path to a path which soon descends steps to the riverside meadows. Here, either go across the stile and follow the riverside path or bear left and follow the tree-lined old ponds across the meadows.

Whichever you choose, you'll arrive at Gibraltar Bridge across the river, which you should now cross. The striking weir, nestling below thickly wooded river cliffs, fed the mill stream of Gibraltar Mill, a textile mill opened in 1760 and demolished in 1967. Fallen masonry, millfloor and hollows litter the wooded area behind the grassy level by the river, while a web of paths lead from the bridge up to the canal. The best way to the tow-path is to take the path immediately left of the low, moss-covered wall opposite the end of the bridge. Climb this to the steps and walled pathway, following this cobble-stoned old trail in turn up to the tow-path and turn right along it.

This is the Lower Peak Forest Canal, opened throughout in 1804 to connect limestone quarries in the northwest Peak District with markets in Manchester. Derelict by the 1930s, it was reopened in 1974, thanks to the work of volunteers and the support of local authorities and now serves as a busy link in the "Cheshire Ring" canal circuit (see the "Up the Etherow" walk for more detail). Many mills took advantage of this form of transport; there is a recently demolished one at the point where the walk joins the tow-path and the still working Unity Mills a little further along for example.

A very pleasant stretch is now in prospect, the canal contouring the well wooded valley side about one hundred feet above the river. The splen-did beech woodlands hide woodpecker, jay, nuthatch and tree-creepers, all living above an undergrowth rich with dog's mercury and ramson. Glimpses through the trees reveal the riverside meadows and old weirs passed earlier before the buildings of Woodley and grit-stone bluffs close in. As old cottages and small warehouses appear on the left, on the right and forlorn in the trees stand the ruins of another old mill, its silted lodges home to alder, hazel and chestnut trees.

Woodley Tunnel cuts 176 yards through one of the area's grit-stone hillsides, unusually keeping the tow-path alongside it – most of these earlier, narrow canals saw canal and tow-path separate at tunnels, the barge horses being led over hill-crests while the boats were "legged" beneath the ground by human power. Beyond the tunnel (take care, the tow-path is a little rough and the roof low – there are railings to keep you out of the water!) remain in the deep cutting for a quarter of a mile or so to the first overbridge (no. 13). Climb the steps on the far side of this and then cross it, following Gilbert Bank up beneath the railway to the corner beside Heald Park Nurseries and the old High Lane farm, its date-stones revealing it was built on 1726.

Turn right with the public footpath sign and walk through the farmyard, ignoring the footpath sign on the left a few paces later. Carry on past the stables and glasshouses and uphill to a stile beside a white-painted metal gate. Once over this, bear left up the narrower, steeper path, a further stile leading to a winding path through a thick stand of gorse bushes, beyond which follow the wall up the hillside towards the old grit-stone farm at the top. Looking back, views from here on a clear day are extensive. To your left (west) the mid-Cheshire ridge and the Clwydian hills in North Wales; sweeping northwards to the West Pennines above Bolton and Bury, the Upper Tame Valley (to the east of the tall hilltop office block in Oldham) and the length of the Dark Peak/South Pennines to the east. More immediately the entire Greater Manchester basin is laid out at your feet.

Cross the stile and bear left along the rough roadway at the top, this side of the grit-stone and mock-Tudor house, almost immediately opening out stunning views across the missing point of the compass. The range of hills stretch from Mow Cop (far right) and Bosley Cloud up along Cheshire's grit-stone edge, Shining Tor to Chinley Churn and the heights of Kinder Scout and Bleaklow. At the far end of the rough lane, turn right down the tarmaced road, Guywood Lane, and follow it to the main road. Turn right here and pass beneath the railway bridge to the station steps, just a few yards beyond which, on the right, is the Railway Inn.

22. Up The Etherow

A walk to explore the lovely, wooded Etherow Valley between Marple, Compstall and Broadbottom in Greater Manchester's south eastern corner, close to the edge of the Peak District.

Distance: 7$^1/_2$ miles (9km)

Map: Landranger 109; Pathfinders 724, 741.

Start: Marple Station (local services on the Manchester – Sheffield line).

Finish: Broadbottom Station (Manchester – Glossop line)

Access: Frequent daily train service from Manchester Piccadilly to Marple Station; return from Broadbottom, regular service (not Sundays) from Broadbottom to Manchester Piccadilly. Day Ranger ticket advised. On Sundays catch bus 214 from back from Broadbottom to Manchester (Tel. 0161 228 7811 for times). Marple is four miles ESE of Stockport on the A626, there is a large car park downhill from the station.

The Pubs

This walk passes by or close to numerous good pubs. At the start of the walk, **The Midland** in Marple Bridge (Whitbread) is beside the river Goyt just one hundred yards downhill from the station. There are several pubs in Compstall, the George and the Andrew Arms (Robinson's) being closest to the route of the walk. In Broadbottom the walk passes no less than five pubs, although my experience is that most don't bother to open on weekday lunchtimes (at least in winter). The exception is **The Station**, ideally situated in terms of this walk as it is, indeed, the old Broadbottom Station building, trains still running past its very door. It's a Banks' house, opened about four years ago following extensive renovation of the long-derelict station; not surprisingly there is a strong railway theme to the decor and fittings, giving something of a Thirties feel with art-deco style glass ceiling and fittings reminiscent of the great European expresses. A variety of bitter and mild are on offer and there's an extensive selection of home cooked food available. Opening hours are 11.30am – 3pm and 5.30pm – 11pm.

Abandoned dye vats at Hodge Fold

The Walk

From the station turn right up the road, Brabyns Brow, then right again along the footpath immediately beyond the telephone box and advertisement hoarding. At the far end, bear left across the wooded pasture, climb the stone steps and turn right along the tow-path of the Lower Peak Forest Canal, reclaimed from dereliction in the years up to its reopening in 1974.

The canal was completed around 1800, at the height of the "Canal Boom" and was built to transport limestone quarried from enormous quarries at (or near) the tiny village of Peak Forest, a couple of miles outside Buxton. Stone from here was transported initially on horse drawn tram-roads, then (from 1831) via a remarkable system of tram-roads, counterbalance railways, inclines and steam lines, together known as the Cromford and High Peak Railway, to Bugsworth and Whaley Bridge canal basins, a few miles southeast of Marple. The eight locks you pass by on this walk are the bottom half of an exhausting (for boat

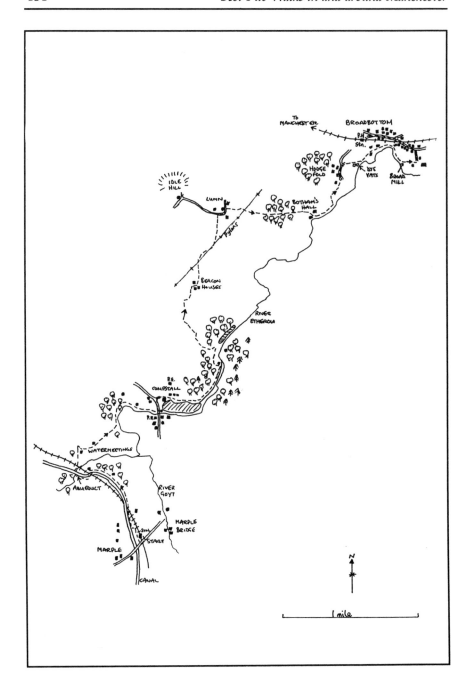

users!) flight of sixteen, dropping the canal through 214 feet – the waterway at the top is the highest currently usable on the entire canal network.

Beyond the bottom lock, cross bridge 16 and continue alongside the canal, pass beneath the viaduct and cross the magnificent Marple Aqueduct, one of the most notable structures on Britain's inland waterways, high above the deep, winding gorge of the river Goyt. Information boards on the tow-path highlight features of this protected, listed structure.

Some fifty yards beyond the aqueduct, turn left off the tow-path to descend the steps and steep path in the woodland, soon passing beneath both aqueduct and parallel railway viaduct. Immediately beyond, follow the line of stiles and waymarked poles or posts half-left to the surfaced farm road and turn right down along this, waymarked as the Valley Way (a yellow arrow on red background with a red heron within the arrow).

Pass by Upper Watermeetings farm, then steer through the farmyard of the Lower Watermeetings farm (the names reflecting the fact that the rivers Goyt and Etherow join together just upstream), following the waymarkers through pastures beyond to gain the river-bank. Turn left and follow the river, by now the Etherow, upstream through pleasant riverside woods to Compstall Bridge (a number of braided paths meander through the woods, simply ensure that whichever you choose to follow, that you're always walking upstream).

Turn left along the road to gain the old market place in Compstall, here bearing right with the sign for the Country Park. Etherow Country Park is based around the watercourses and reservoirs created to serve the Compstall Mills complex, a part of which survives alongside the substantial lake. The mills – and, indeed, many of the now highly-prized village terraces – were built for George Andrew from the 1820s onwards; his spinning, weaving and calico printing concerns, such as the Albert and Victoria Mills, employed nearly a thousand people at their height before finally closing in 1966.

The lake supplied large water-wheels – one, christened "Lily," was claimed to be, at fifty feet in diameter, the largest in the country – the water for the succeeding steam boilers and the immense quantities were needed in the washing and bleaching processes. It's now a noted site for waterfowl, both summer migrants and overwintering flocks, detailed on static boards and in the excellent Visitor Centre.

If you're ready for refreshment, then there are several possibilities in Compstall, the Andrew Arms on George Street (just above the Visitor Centre) for example is a pleasant, traditional village local offering Robinson's beers.

From the Visitor Centre, take the narrow lake-side path (the water to your right) and follow this up the wooded valley for half a mile alongside the mill leat above the river. This ends in an open grassy area, at the far end of which is the magnificent weir across the Etherow which supplies the leat. The mill leat served a dual purpose, acting both as feeder to the great lake and as a canal along which iron tub-boats (one survives alongside the leat) plied, carrying coal from small pits in and around the local woodland, valley sides and tops to the industrial complex at Compstall. At least one of these small pits remained active (worked by one man) until the early 1970s.

Don't cross the bridge below the weir, instead turn back through the open space and take the road up and right (follow the toilets sign) winding along behind the house and through the woodland, resplendent with myriad wild flowers in spring and early summer. These woods were developed as a shooting reserve by the Andrew family and are now, in complete contrast, a nature reserve. In about a quarter of a mile, turn left up along the path signposted for the Valley Way (beside the wooden shelter) and wind with this out of the steep, wooded Mortin Clough through a gate. Cross the double stile, go immediately over a further stile on your right and walk up to the fingerpost. Turn right and follow the lane through the gaggle of houses at Beacon Houses and beyond along the contour. Excellent views open out across the deep valley of the Etherow to the heights of Ludworth Moor beyond.

Pass beneath the line of electricity pylons and, about 150 metres beyond this point, climb the stile beside a gate on your right, then follow the line of pylons across the field to a small wooden stile. Cross this and bear slightly left, away from the line of pylons, contour walking across several fields, following the line of ruined wall across the last one to a stone stile beside a field gate leading to a minor road.

If it's a very clear day and you're feeling energetic, then turn left uphill and walk up the steep road to the top. From the car park beside the pub here on Idle Hill are massive views across Manchester to the West Pennine Moors, across the Cheshire Plain to the Berwyns in North Wales and across the rolling moors into Yorkshire and Derbyshire. Otherwise, turn right down the lane and follow it downhill and left. Opposite the cream-painted bungalow on your left, go right along the signposted footpath beneath the thick bower of old holly trees.

Cross the farm road and continue down the old sunken track. At the end, bear half right along the rough road and follow it round through the pasture. Climb the stile to the right of the field gate, walk to the left of the small oak tree, enter the woods then follow the well defined path down through these woods, home to a wealth of birds, including nuthatch, tree creepers and jays.

Near the foot of the woods, cross the brook and bear right, again picking up the Valley Way signpost. Go through the yard of Bothams Hall and remain with the rough lane beyond, eventually reaching the hamlet of Hodge Fold. Follow the lane up past Hodge Fold Cottages to the point where the tarmaced lane bends left. Here, continue ahead (with the Valley Way waymark), keeping right at the next junction. A few yards further along are the solid remains of a series of dye vats, a remarkable series of deep grit-stone troughs in which cloth was bleached and dyed, possibly as late as 1913 when the local print-works eventually closed after more than a century of service. Walk-ways and viewing platforms make studying the site, and the riverside settling tanks, easy.

Continue along Hodge Lane, passing by a series of marshy or dried up millponds. The large house perched in woodland beyond the last of these, off to your left is Hodge House, once home to the Matley family, owners of the print-works. Beyond this point the lane rises steeply to pass by a fine terrace of three-storey weavers' cottages, the top storey still retaining several gallery-windows, so-designed to let in the maximum of light to allow the piecework or jobbing weavers the maximum working day.

Virtually at the far end of these, pass through the gateway on the right (waymarked) and follow this narrow path above cottage gardens and into woodland. The path descends steeply to the near end of a row of substantial grit-stone terraces, Well Row. Turn right here and trace the path alongside the safety rail to the footbridge at the bottom. Don't cross this; rather, pass through the kissing gate and enter the great area of ruins that mark the site of Broad Mill. Keep right to join the riverside path and continue through the complex, information boards here and there outlining the history of the site and the function of particular buildings.

Ignore the path which rises, left, immediately beyond the site of the old water-wheel pit, favouring instead the path which emerges from the trees at the edge of a great open space dotted with further remains, including the base of an old gasholder. A board at the entrance gate outlines the history of this part of the site. Beyond here follow the roadway to the terrace of brick cottages and turn left up the rough Lymefield road, still graced by gas-lamp standards. The low, modern building on your right is Lymefield Visitor Centre (open weekends only). At the top of Lymefield, turn left along Lower Market Street, pass beneath the railway bridge and continue uphill along the main road to arrive at the station approach road, beside the old goods and engine shed on your left. The Station is just beyond the car park here.

23. The Mersey Valley

A walk from East Didsbury along the broad valley of the River Mersey taking in Stenner Woods, Broad Ees Dole and Priory Gardens, a valley as rich in local as natural history.

Distance: 7 miles (11km)

Maps: Landranger Sheet 109; Pathfinders 723, 724.

Start: East Didsbury Station (BR)

Finish: Dane Road Station (Metrolink)

Access: East Didsbury is six miles south of Manchester City Centre on the A34; the walk starts near the Tesco store, where on-street parking is usually possible – alternatively park at any Metrolink Station going outward via Piccadilly to take the train to East Didsbury, returning via Metrolink to your car. Regular trains run every day from Piccadilly to East Didsbury, many Airport trains also call here. Frequent Metrolink trams return from Dane Road to the City Centre, Altrincham and beyond.

The Pubs

The route of this walk passes two interesting pubs as it meanders along the Mersey Valley. **The Olde Cock Inn** is on the edge of Didsbury Village, facing what was once the village green. It's a Whitbread "Free House" offering Boddington's, Castle Eden and a wide variety of guest beers; it occasionally also hosts a mini beer festival. The name reflects the once popular "sport" of cock fighting which was practiced in the vicinity; bull baiting was also noted on the village green. The pub itself is probably over three centuries old, hung with an enormous number of prints and old photographs. Its capacious interior is hugely popular with students from the nearby university college. It's open all day and bar meals are usually available.

The second pub is the isolated **Jackson's Boat**, at one end of a footbridge across the river. Jackson is assumed to have been the operator of a chain ferry which crossed the Mersey at this point; other names the pub has gone under during the past three hundred years or so include the Greyhound, the Bridge and the Church. It's a Tetley house, with Tetley Bitter and Jenning's Bitter on hand-pump. Within, a central bar serves both open plan area and umpteen alcoves, outside is a tree shaded patio and beer garden. Afternoon closing is 3pm.

The Walk

From the southbound platform (which trains from Manchester use), walk down the station approach and turn left beneath the bridge. At the traffic lights turn left along Parrswood Road and follow this to its very end, a few yards past a row of shops on your right. Beyond these walk ahead along the narrow Millgate Lane, staying with this to reach the Old Bedians sports club on your left. At this juncture, locate the stile on your right and walk across the wooden causeway laid to ease passage across the marshy ground beside a small pond, then climb the bank and turn left.

Down to the left is Millgate Farm, its name suggesting a former mill in the vicinity, although no remains exist and its very location is uncertain; one reason being that the Mersey was prone to alter its channel as it meandered across its wide flood plain, thus any mill race – and even the mill itself – will have been destroyed and reconstructed several times over the centuries. At the sharp left hand bend, look to your right for a ruined stile beside the gate, climb this and bear slightly left, following the line of fence up across the pasture to a further stile, cross over and turn left.

Turn right when you reach the river. Near here, where Millgate Lane once petered out, was the site of Gatley Ford (actually on the far side of the motorway whose construction necessitated the re-routing of the river). Once one of the main passages from the south into Manchester, it is recorded that at least part of Bonnie Prince Charlie's army forded the river here in 1745 as they advanced south towards London. Weeks later, fleeing in disarray from failure at Derby, they again made use of the crossing.

Follow the river downstream, its course dictated by massive embank-ments built during the 1970s as the latest attempt to alleviate the flooding to which the river was prone. Such flood control measures were first recorded as long ago as the thirteenth century when marshy

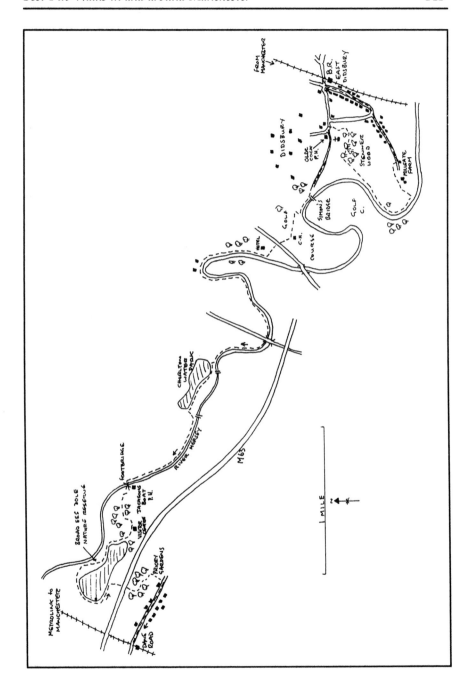

riverside pastures were enclosed and improved in the Didsbury area. To reach this section, stay on the riverside path. About a hundred yards past the point where the immature woodland has been planted on the flood bank, and where a straight section of river reveals a view to housing in the distance, bear right off the riverside path to find a wide path leading to a red metal field gate across the path. Continue along the path past this, woodland now on your right.

This is Stenner Wood, and it has its entrance at the far end. Go through the gate here on your right into the trees and follow the path along the inner edge, lined by oaks and chestnuts. This old woodland is perhaps the largest tract left in the lower Mersey Valley in Greater Manchester. The path winds round to a gap stile beneath a stand of massive willow trees. Remain within the trees and turn right along the path along an embankment. This leads to a series of board-walks (on the left near the far end of the wood) which snake above the boggy woodland floor and ponds (keep right at the split), to emerge at the edge of parkland. Walk along the edge of this to find the cafe (summer only) and conveniences, adjoining the Rock Garden and Alpine House, an integral part of Didsbury's renowned Fletcher Moss Botanical Gardens.

At your leisure work your way along the surfaced path past the upper tennis courts to gain the main road and turn left to the Olde Cock Inn, overlooking what was once the village green. Immediately to the left of the pub, the ornate gate leads into the gardens surrounding The Old Parsonage, a part of the Botanical Gardens. This was home to the eponymous Fletcher Moss, an Alderman of the City of Manchester, renowned antiquarian and local benefactor for many years (he gave the Gardens to the City) until his death early this century. He established and nurtured the gardens, their southerly aspect being suitable for growing sub-tropical species as well as alpine plants; there's also an orchid house with over one hundred different species on display. Entry is free.

Leave the Gardens via the gate opposite the village church. St James' originates from around 1235, possibly on the site of a Saxon church (the name Didsbury is held to derive from Diddles Burgh, burgh being a Saxon word for a defended site). The current building is somewhat more recent and contains the Mosley Chapel, named after the local family of that name, one of whom was the British Fascist leader, Sir Oswald Mosley. A notice pinned to the board beside the lychgate proclaims that the door to God's House is never closed... but presumably fear of vandalism or theft makes this no longer possible.

Walk down Stenner Lane, past the terrace of old cottages and ahead at the crossing of lanes, following the tarmaced by-way to the car park at the far end. Here, climb the steps on your left to rejoin the river embankment, turning right along this. The footbridge, Simon's Bridge (named after the Simon family, Lords of Wythenshawe), dates from 1901 when it replaced a shallow ford. Until the inter-war period, a popular local excursion was by a small steamboat which plied between Northenden and Simon's Bridge. Don't cross it, instead remain on the embankment for a further hundred yards or so to the bend in the river. Here look down to the right for the footpath giving access to the golf course fairway. Follow the narrow path, hedge to your left, along to the new clubhouse at Withington golf club.

Climb the steps and bear right alongside the building, crossing straight over the busy road just a few yards away and continue along the subsequent path. Cross the hotel's driveway, climb the steps over the embankment and turn downstream. For the next mile and more, simply follow the great curves of the river, eventually passing beneath the three bridges at Princess Road. The oldest, central span dates only from the 1920s, built as part of the initial development of Wythenshawe, turning this ancient hamlet into one of the first of the "Garden City" developments, though perhaps Ebeneezer Howard's planned cities of Letchworth and Welwyn Garden City to the north of London are generally better known.

A short while after passing these bridges, a green-painted bailey bridge crosses the river. Don't cross, but turn right here to gain the shore of the lake at Chorlton Water Park, following the path a few yards above the water to your right. The lake is flooded gravel diggings used in the construction of the nearby M63 motorway in the 1970s; it now has a growing reputation as a fishery and attracts a goodly number of waterbirds, particularly during the winter. At the far end of the water, pass through the stile beside the gate on your left and walk ahead across the old access road to rejoin the river, again turning downstream.

The embankments, somewhat bare during the winter, are luxuriant in summer with wild flowers which include comfrey, willowherb, butterbur, balsam and bugloss, offering splurges of colour for months on end.

Follow the riverside or embankment-top path to the footbridge at Jackson's Boat, nearly a mile downstream, which replaced the eponymous ferry nearly two hundred years ago. Cross this to the pub on the far bank.

To demonstrate the Mersey's shifting course over the years, the pub was (until the local government changes in 1974 saw the creation of Greater Manchester) always seen as being in Lancashire despite being on the south (Cheshire) bank of the waterway; the Mersey traditionally being accepted as the Lancashire/Cheshire boundary. When originally built and licensed, the building was north of the river, but its course shifted as floods altered the lineation of the natural banks.

Refreshed, walk to the far end of the pub car park (the one opposite the pub, not the one behind it), bear left up the path and pick up the bank-top path, shortly descending to the right. At the gate go straight ahead (please ignore the gate into the model aircraft club field), after one hundred yards or so, take the path on the left through the scrubby woodland in the nature reserve. At the far side, bear right to the tall modern building.

This is the Mersey Valley Visitor Centre, worth spending some time at as there are ever-changing interpretive displays and friendly, knowledgeable staff well versed in the flora and fauna of the Valley; there's also a cafe and toilet facilities. The Centre is open daily except Mondays, a regularly updated information board details which species of birds and mammals are currently in the area.

Take the path which descends from the front of the Centre (NOT the car park side) and joins the narrow tarmaced lane, until the 1970s a rough cart track called Cow Lane. Following this soon has you at the shore-line of Sale Water Park, another lake developed in old gravel workings. Follow the shore-line, the water on your left; the harsh building on the far bank is the watersport centre, restaurant and bar. A waterside stroll takes you to a bird hide overlooking what was, until 1972, Withington Sewage Works. Reclaimed, planted and managed, the site is now a renowned wildfowl and bird-watching site, well over one hundred species having been recorded here. The reed-beds, channels and marshes complement the main lake, home to great flocks of Canada geese during the winter, together with cormorants and herons. Animals to look out for include foxes and wild mink and, late on summer evenings, bats.

Didsbury's St James' church, high above the flood meadows of the Mersey

Keep to the path around the head of the lake, passing the sluice tower on your left. About one hundred yards past this, opposite the second lifebelt holder, look right for a set of wooden steps set in the embankment, leading up to an underpass beneath the motorway. Once through this, walk ahead following the trail of "4" posts into Priory Woods. Sale Priory once stood here; a former owner stipulated in her will that, when pronounced dead, her body should be kept above ground for a hundred years and regularly inspected to ensure that she was, indeed, dead!

Pass a couple of large houses off to your right and then take any one of the several paths down, right, through the wooded hollow and up to the main road on the far side. Turn right along this and walk along to Dane Road station about 250 metres away for trams back into central Manchester or, if you're dying of thirst, continue the few extra paces over the Bridgewater Canal to the Bridge Inn (Boddington's, open all day).

24. Broadoak

An attractive circular walk from High Lane via Hawk Green and Norbury Hollow almost on the fringe of the ancient forest of Macclesfield and Derbyshire's Peak District.

Distance: around 7 miles (10km)

Maps: Landranger 109, Pathfinder 741.

Start and Finish: The Bull's Head, High Lane. Grid reference SJ 951853

Access: The Bull's Head is beside the A6 in High Lane, about five miles SE of Stockport. There is a small pub car park here, alternatively use the public car park on the left a few yards beyond (east of) the canal bridge or one of the village side roads. Regular daily buses run from Stockport through High Lane (e.g. 198/9, 361); tel. 0161 228 7811 for timetable information. Alternatively take a train to Middlewood on the Piccadilly-Buxton line – a public path leads from the station via the Middlewood Way northeastwards by a track to High Lane. Turn right at the A6 for the Canal and Bull's Head – distance approximately half a mile. The return part of the walk passes close by the station.

The Pub

A large number of pubs survive along the old coaching route between Manchester and Buxton, and the **Bull's Head** is one of the best of them. The inn benefited not only from passing road traffic, but also boat traffic on the Macclesfield Canal, beside which the pub stands. It's nominally a Boddington's house, but in addition to this house bitter, it also offers guest beers such as Marston's Pedigree and Taylor's Landlord. One small bar serves the main room, off which are a couple of snugs and all have low beams and are comfortably appointed. At the rear of the pub a quiet patio area carries tables and benches overlooking the often busy canal. The pub is open all day (standard Sunday hours) and bar food is available.

Windlehurst Deer Farm

The Walk

From the patio behind the Bull's Head join the tow-path and walk north, the Macclesfield Canal is to your right. The Canal was opened as late as 1831 to facilitate transport of textiles from Manchester to the markets of the Midlands, pottery from Stoke to the great markets of Manchester and its satellite towns and to serve the little known East Cheshire coalfield at Poynton. Despite competition from rail (the essentially parallel Macclesfield, Bollington and Marple line opened in 1869), the canal remained profitable and heavily used well into this century and now forms part of the "Cheshire Ring" canal circuit, one of the busiest on the inland waterways network.

Beyond the second overbridge, the rough wooded area on the right marks the site of Windlehurst Mill. This cotton spinning mill was built in 1872 but beset with misfortune; it burned down in about 1899, was rebuilt and then in 1908 was wrecked by a freak whirlwind. Left to decay for a number of years, the site was eventually cleared and planted

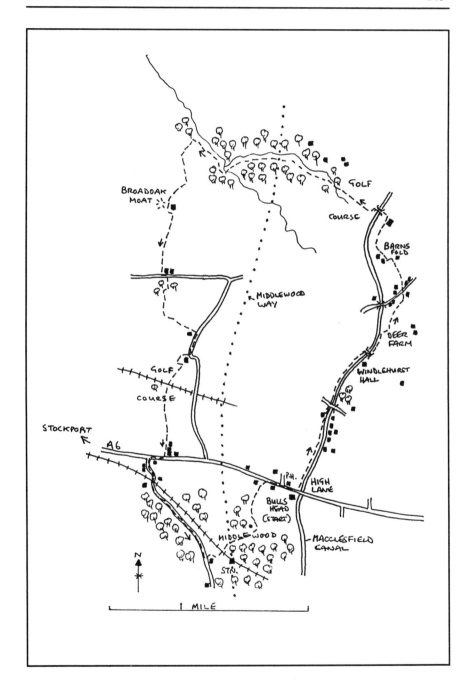

with the trees there today, the only reminders of the mill, an important local employer, are a few blocks of masonry.

Again on the right, just yards before the next overbridge, are the tumbledown ruins of Windlehurst Hall, a mansion built during Victoria's reign for the wealthy owner of a successful Manchester jewellery business but derelict now these many years. Cross the canal bridge (No. 8) here and turn left along the canal-side path. The fields down to the right are parkland grazed by a substantial herd of deer, managed strictly for their meat and hides rather than any aesthetic pleasure. In many ways this farming practice mirrors the use to which the land hereabouts was used centuries ago, as a deer park to provide hunting for the Lords of the Manor and royalty.

Cross the stile some yards before the next bridge (essentially above the far end of the deer pastures) and bear half-right to a further stile. Cross directly over the farm road and walk up to the right of the hedge opposite. Cross a further stile and wind round with the tall thorn and holly hedge, keeping it, and the small pumping station, on your left. Pass through the wide gap in the cross-hedge, thence bear half-right across the pasture and walk towards the old white cottage. On a clear day the views across the Manchester basin to the City Centre and the West Pennine Moors beyond are extensive. Climb the stile by the cottage, walk along the driveway to the main road, then take the path virtually opposite (well hidden between the white houses and the dormer bungalow) marked by a Holly Trail way-marker.

Persevere with this sometimes tortuously narrow path for about 300 yards, climb the stile and walk between the lines of cupressus trees to the narrow road, turning left along this. In about 40 yards bear right with the Holly Trail logo and signpost and walk through the gravelled yard beside the solid old grit-stone farmhouse, one of a number of pleasing buildings in this tiny hamlet, known as Barns Fold. Continue along the track, pass alongside the left of the warehouse and turn left to the canal. Cross this and turn left, then right at the waymark (a rambler with a walking stick) and walk down across the golf course.

Cross several fairways to reach a spinney, then follow the Holly Trail waymarks, the origin of its name immediately obvious. At the far end of the golf course cross the old railway (now the Middlewood Way bridle-path and cycleway) and take the fenced path opposite, soon dropping down into the wooded dingle of Torkington Brook. Cross the green footbridge and climb the steep path to another golf course.

Turn right towards Offerton, skirting the trees. Walk down the steps, cross the plank bridge and go left towards Torkington Road. Follow the waymarks to a further plank bridge and eventually the stile to the left of the small pond. Walk to the hedge about 50 yards away and turn right to Broadoak Farm.

This site dates back to medieval times. In 1354 it was recorded that John de Legh enclosed from the Royal Forest of Macclesfield ("Forest" being land subject to draconian laws imposed by the sovereign to protect his hunting lands rather than a forest of trees as we use the word today) some sixty acres and built a moated house there. Only the substantial watery moat now remains, yet another reminder of the powerful Legh family whose properties are dotted all over north-eastern Cheshire (Lyme Hall and Park, and Adlington Hall for example).

Pass between the farm and the moat, turn left at the far end of the buildings, then right along the long driveway to the road. Enter the field virtually opposite and cross the stream. Turn right at the waymark to reach a signpost, here turn left and go through the farmyard to a minor road. Turn right and continue to the sharp bend at the drive to Dean Fold House. Follow the direction indicated by the footpath sign here and trace the outside of the garden fence to the corner. Turn left (signposted Middlewood Way) to a further signpost virtually behind the house, finally turning right here across a golf fairway.

Head for High Lane, across the railway bridge and further fairways towards the squat aerial on the near horizon, then along the hedged track-way near the 11th tee to join the A6 road. Turn right, then left along Norbury Hollow Road, remaining with this quiet, wooded back-road, cobbled for much of its initial length, for about half a mile beyond the level crossing. Pass by a pair of stone gateposts on your left, marking the entrance to Norbury Hollow Cottage, then in a few yards look down for a footbridge across the brook. Cross this and walk ahead to cross the drive, then turn right through the black gate and walk along to the end of the pasture.

Climb the steep steps on the left and cross the extant railway (take care, it is busy with passenger and heavy freight trains) to gain the woods.

Follow the board-walk, cross the brook and walk up to the line of the old railway, the Middlewood Way. Go straight over this and into Middle Wood itself, a favourite spot for day-trippers right up until the 1950s. Pass by the cottage on your left and wind along with the track to the A6 some distance away, turning right to return to the Bull's Head.

Immediately before reaching the pub, the warehouse restaurant and small boat-yard on your right mark the site of Norbury basin. A century ago this was a thriving undertaking, busy with coal brought in both via tram-road from the nearby Norbury Pit and boated in from the main coalfield a mile or so to the south.

25. Ladybrook

Bramall Hall and Poynton Pool are two of the attractions on this interesting walk on the edge of Stockport out to Middlewood, utilising the Ladybrook Valley Way for part of the way.

Distance: 7 miles (11km)

Maps: Landranger 109, Pathfinder 741.

Start: Cheadle Hulme Station

Finish: Middlewood Station

Access: Frequent trains from Manchester Piccadilly call at Cheadle Hulme (Hazel Grove local services); trains every two hours (Monday – Saturday), hourly on Sundays return from Middlewood to Piccadilly (Buxton line); alternative bus services operate along the A6 (half a mile from the station) to Stockport and Manchester. Check times (0161 228 7811) before departure. The Cheadle Hulme pub is next to the station, 3 miles SW of Stockport town centre; there's a large car park nearby. Motorists should park at Stockport.

The Pub

The Cheadle Hulme was moulded from the shell of The Junction Inn, built in the 1840s to serve the newly arrived railway. The present pub has little in common with the original – brewers' Joseph Holt, having expanded and modernised the pub extensively – but the pub continues to offer excellently kept mild and bitter at Holts' gratifyingly low prices (bitter at 96 pence a pint, March 1994). The cavernous interior houses a comfortable general bar (open all day) and a separate dining area.

The Walk

From the pub walk beneath the two railway bridges, and immediately turn right along the driveway beside Pimlotts' butchers, which drive also gives access to one of the station platforms. Continue along the fenced path which parallels the foot of the railway embankment, eventually issuing some half mile later onto a main road. Turn right along this and

then right again in a matter of a hundred yards or so, along the footpath
adorned with a "Ladybrook Valley" sign-board.

Pass beneath the railway viaduct, through the squeezer stile and follow
the meandering brook upstream. A surprisingly peaceful walk is now in
prospect, flat water meadows filling the valley floor between the con-
siderably higher river terraces which hide the surrounding suburbs.
Massive crack-willow trees line Ladybrook, oak, alder, sycamore and the
odd Corsican pine dot rougher pastureland which once hosted small
clay diggings, long returned to nature. Bricks were the main product of
such industry and a typical fine old Cheshire-brick house graces the
slopes a little north of the brook.

The only man-made feature of note is a narrow stone bridge erected in
1897 to commemorate Queen Victoria's Diamond Jubilee. The brook
tumbles over artificial rapids and small weirs, the result of flood control
schemes this century rather than the start of old mill leats; the valley
hosted surprisingly few mills in the section visited on this walk.

Further on the valley becomes increasingly constricted and the well-
to-do suburb of Bramhall comes to dominate the valley crest above and
amongst the mature oak and sycamore of Manor Wood before the path
reaches a main road. Cross straight over this to enter the landscaped
parkland surrounding Bramall Hall. Walk ahead to the first pond and
skirt this to the left, the brook meandering down to your left. At the end
of the pond, leave the Ladybrook Valley Way and bear right, climbing
steps to reach the courtyard of the old Hall.

Dating from around 1400, Bramall Hall was one of the homes of the
Davenport family who remained in residence until 1877. It's one of the
largest "Magpie Houses" in England, much of the current structure
dating from the time of Shakespeare (late 1500s-early 1600s), a veritable
fairytale of leaded windows, gables, structural timbers dipping at odd
angles, huge chimney breasts topped by ornate brick chimneys and a
glorious inner courtyard. Inside are medieval wall paintings and rooms
large and small furnished with period pieces. In 1925 there was the
distinct possibility that the whole structure be transported to the U.S.A.
and re-erected in New England (a fate that befell a number of stately
homes during the twenties and thirties); fortunately the plan fell through
and the hall remained *in situ*, passing eventually to the care of the
Borough Council who maintain it today. Opening times vary, essentially

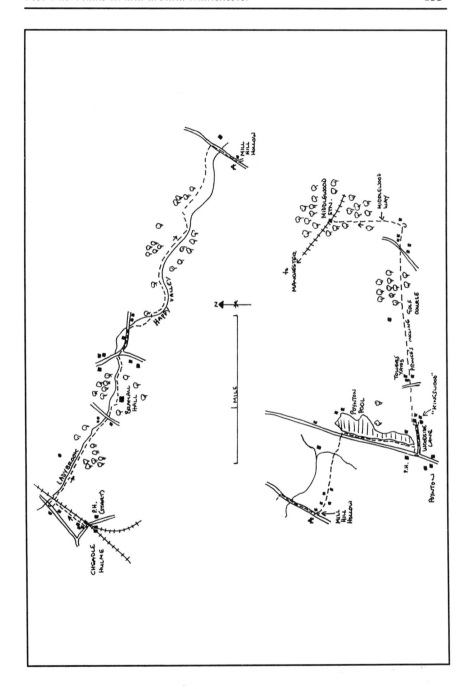

weekend afternoons only January-March, every afternoon April-September, closed Mondays October-December. There is an entry charge. Details on 0161-485 3708.

Once you've seen the Hall your way lies eastwards through the Park, either along the main drive or by rejoining the Ladybrook Valley Way and following the brook upstream. Either way you'll join a busy main road at the end of the Park. Cross this road and bear right towards the traffic roundabout, taking the first exit left from this, the A5143 for Macclesfield. In about one hundred yards, cross this to regain the riverside path at Womanscroft Bridge, a section of the route known as Happy Valley. One of the old valley mills is thought to have been here, but records on the subject are vague and remains non-existent.

Walking upstream, cross the wooden footbridge beneath the massive willow and turn right along the far bank, following this fenced path into the great bowl the brook has created in the landscape. This is a peaceful stretch, the brook, braided here and there with gravelly shoals, banks and small islets, meandering beneath overhangs of deep red sandstone and lined with great old willows and alders. The pastures and hay-meadows are dotted with copses and huge old oak, elm and ash trees, with Highland cattle possibly grazing here during summer months.

In a while the valley constricts again, having cut a shallow gorge in the sandstone in the shadow of a beech-capped knoll. Here climb the stile, then, in twenty yards or so, cross the slab footbridge on your right and follow the path beyond along the break of slope between the knoll and hay-meadows. The next half mile opens out distant views to the Peak District beyond an ancient, white-painted farmhouse.

On gaining the road turn right and cross the river bridge, here entering Cheshire for much of the remainder of the walk. Continue uphill for fifty or so yards and bear left along Mill Hill Hollow, following this back lane to its end at the house called Coppice End. Follow the narrow path to the left of this house, climb the stile at the end and continue along, following in part the scant remains of an old mill leat which once supplied a mill hereabouts. Follow the path to and over the footbridge across a limpid stretch of water. This once provided the head of water to the afore-mentioned mill and, possibly, helped drive a dynamo to light the house and grounds of Barlowfold House (off to your left), one of the first in Stockport to have electricity.

At ease in Happy Valley – a Highland Cow chews the cud in Stockport's rural hinterland

The path leads to the very busy A523 trunk road; go directly over this and up the steps opposite to the shore-line of the large Poynton Pool, turn right along this. The landscaped acres on the far side are Poynton Park, once the demesne of "The Towers," country mansion of the Vernon family, Earls of Derby and owners of many of the collieries in the little known Cheshire coalfield which once thrived hereabouts. The origin of Boycott Pool is subject to argument, some claim it is purely an artificial parkland feature while others suggest it is flooded workings first excavated to provide ballast for the then new turnpike road, the current A523.

Walk to the end of the pool and turn right to the junction with the main road, at the corner of which is one of the old lodge-houses to the long demolished "Towers." If you've worked up a thirst by now, then turn right to find the Bulls Head, a fine Boddington's establishment. Otherwise turn left along the main road, then left again up Woodside Lane, following this to its end. Go to the left of the "Kingswood" sign and left again outside the estate wall, following the signpost for "Prince's Incline, Middlewood Way and Canal."

The long, straight, gradual slope you now ascend was one of the inclines serving coal mines in the area. Loaded wagons descended the slope, connected via ropes and pulleys to empty wagons which were thus hauled up to the collieries as a counterbalance; connecting lines took wagons on to interchange sidings at Poynton main line station. Prince's Incline was named after Queen Victoria's Consort, as was one of the mines it served, Albert Pit. Stick with the old incline across Towers Road, immediately after which are buildings contemporary with the collieries; on the left the manager's office and cashier's office, on the right part of the old stables where some of the hundred and more pit ponies may occasionally have rested.

Further reminders of the coalfield dot the landscape as you slowly gain height. The incline becomes a more obvious feature, off to the left are the remains of Park Pits, once the largest on the coalfield and the last to be closed, in 1935. On reaching the corner beside the golfing green, cross the farm access road and take the narrow path, initially with a fence to your left, up into the woods. This is still the incline. Remain with it to cross the tarmaced road, beyond which the rough road is named as Prince Road. Off to the right from here is visible the only substantial spoil tip which remains, at the old Anson Pit.